AIR CAMPAIGN

MALAYA & DUTCH EAST INDIES 1941–42

Japan's air power shocks the world

MARK STILLE | ILLUSTRATED BY JIM LAURIER

OSPREY PUBLISHING
Bloomsbury Publishing Plc
PO Box 883, Oxford, OX1 9PL, UK
1385 Broadway, 5th Floor, New York, NY 10018, USA
Email: info@ospreypublishing.com
www.ospreypublishing.com

OSPREY is a trademark of Osprey Publishing Ltd

First published in Great Britain in 2020

A catalog record for this book is available from the British Library.

ISBN: PB 9781472840592; eBook 9781472840608;
ePDF 9781472840578; XML 9781472840585

20 21 22 23 24 10 9 8 7 6 5 4 3 2 1

Maps by www.bounford.com
Battlescenes by Jim Laurier
3D BEVs by Paul Kime
Index by Fionbar Lyons
Typeset by PDQ Digital Media Solutions, Bungay, UK
Printed and bound in India by Replika Press Private Ltd.

Editor's note
Andrew Thomas' photos are thanks to the extensive collection of the late P. H. T. Green, the late Air Cdre E. W. Wright, the late J. A. Campbell, the late J. Bury, the late Alan Richardson and the 64th Sentai Association.

CONTENTS

INTRODUCTION

This is an impressive September 1941 photograph of 243 Squadron in flight with its Buffalo fighters. Note the aircraft are grouped in sections of three with a leader and two wingmen. RAF fighter pilots had little respect for their Japanese counterparts before the war, born from near-total ignorance of their potential enemy. When hostilities began, it was quickly apparent that RAF fighter pilots were stuck flying an inferior aircraft. (Library of Congress)

When the European powers went to war in September 1939, the Far East remained a backwater. But the quiet in this part of the world was only temporary. The Japanese Empire had already embarked on a policy of expansion having annexed Manchuria in 1931 and invaded China in 1937. Operations in China were indecisive but the obvious intent of the Japanese to impose their domination over China by increasingly brutal means increased tensions between the United States and Japan. In 1940, the Germans conquered the Netherlands and France and put Great Britain under direct threat of invasion. This presented the Japanese with an opportunity to insulate themselves from increasing economic pressure from the United States. The resource-rich colonial possessions of the European powers in the Far East lay open to attack. French Indochina was a rich source of rice and provided an ideal staging point to attack the other European possessions in the Far East. The Federated Malay States under British control was a source of much of the world's tin and rubber and had considerable oil resources; the Netherlands East Indies (NEI) was oil rich.

The Japanese advance into Southeast Asia was the most important operation in the series of Japanese attacks in the opening months of the war. Contrary to Allied expectations, the Japanese were able to conduct multiple thrusts concurrently. The strongest Allied forces in the region were the British air, naval, and ground forces in Malaya and Singapore. Additionally, American forces in the Philippines had to be neutralized. Once this had been accomplished, the assault on the NEI could begin. Seizure of the NEI was most important to the Japanese from a resource perspective, and this had to be done quickly before the Dutch could comprehensively destroy the oil facilities or the Americans or British could introduce reinforcements.

The entire Japanese plan was largely based on the successful application of air power. Allied ground forces in the region outnumbered the relatively small Imperial Army forces committed to the operation. The decisive edge for the Japanese was in air power where they held a significant advantage over British, Dutch, and American forces. Gaining air superiority would permit the Japanese to fully exploit their superior naval forces. For the conquest of

Malaya, the attack was supported primarily by the Imperial Japanese Army Air Force (IJAAF) with the Imperial Japanese Navy Air Force (IJNAF) playing a supporting role. The IJAAF planned to destroy British air power in northern Malaya in a classic offensive counterair campaign lasting only a few days.

British defense planning in the Far East was also built around air power. The centerpiece of the British position in the region was the naval base at Singapore and the assumption was that it would receive a large fleet soon after hostilities opened with Japan. This assumption turned out to be invalid when conditions in Europe extended the time it would take the Royal Navy (RN) to dispatch a fleet to the Far East. The size of the British Army in Malaya was insufficient to repel a Japanese invasion; this left the Royal Air Force (RAF) as the principal defender of British interests in the Far East. Even with this realization, the RAF in the Far East was not prepared for war. It lacked sufficient aircraft to perform its missions of defending the naval base at Singapore and seriously weakening a Japanese seaborne invasion force. Most of the aircraft assigned to the Far East were obsolescent. Also, although in the middle of a large-scale expansion when the Pacific War began, the RAF did not possess an adequate infrastructure to withstand a Japanese attack. This lack of sufficient modern aircraft and the supporting infrastructure for air defense would have severe consequences in the forthcoming campaign.

The Japanese campaign to occupy the NEI was even more dependent on air power since the Japanese would have to seize a series of airfields on various islands to support their leapfrog advance. This campaign was supported almost exclusively by the IJNAF. Facing the Japanese was a mixed bag of Allied air units, including the Dutch East Indies Air Squadron with a combination of Dutch, German, and American-designed and supplied aircraft. The United States Army Air Force (USAAF) also sent significant, but ultimately inadequate, numbers of aircraft to Java, the main island in the NEI and the ultimate objective of the Japanese. The RAF fell back to airfields on Sumatra in the NEI in the last stages of the Malaya campaign, and was involved in the final stages of the campaign to defend the NEI. For the same reason that the Allied air campaign failed in Malaya, the effort to defend the NEI was also futile.

CHRONOLOGY

1941

December 8 Japanese make coordinated landings at Singora and Patani in southern Thailand and at Kota Bharu in northern Malaya

Japanese make first raid on Singapore and begin a series of raids against British airfields in northern Malaya

December 9 Japanese seize Kota Bharu airfield

Second day of air combat shatters British air power in northern Malaya

December 10 Battleship *Prince of Wales* and battlecruiser *Repulse* sunk by Japanese air attack

December 11 British fighters withdrawn to defend Singapore and supply convoys giving Japanese air superiority over northern Malaya

Battle for Jitra results in a major British defeat leading to the loss of northern Malaya

December 14 Japanese capture Alor Star Airfield virtually intact

December 16 Japanese land at Miri, British Borneo

December 19 RAF abandons Ipoh Airfield

December 25 Japanese capture Jolo in central NEI

December 31 British ground commander ordered to hold airfields in central Malaya long enough to allow the arrival of several reinforcement convoys

1942

January 3 British abandon Kuantan Airfield

IJN bases
Allied naval bases
Hainan
THAILAND
INDOCHINA
South China Sea
Cam Ranh Bay
Saigon
Lingayen Gulf
Luzon
Clark Field
Bataan Peninsula
Manila
Cavite
Manila Bay
Corregidor
Legaspi
Panay
PHILIPPINES
Sulu Sea
Del Monte
Davao
Palau Island
Jolo
Singora
Kota Bharu
Penang
MALAY STATES
Kuantan
Endau
Singapore
Sumatra
NORTH BORNEO
BRUNEI
Miri
SARAWAK
Kuching
Celebes Sea
Tarakan
Menado
Kema
Moluccas
NETHERLANDS EAST INDIES
Borneo
Balikpapan
Makassar Strait
Celebes
Banjarmasin
Kendari
Makassar
Bangka Strait
Bangka Island
Palembang
Gaspar Strait
Java Sea
Bawean Island
Bantam Bay
Tandjong Priok
Sunda Strait
Batavia
Bandoeng
Madoera
Surabaja
Java
Tjilatjap
Bali
Denpesar
Bali Strait
Badoeng Strait
Lombok
Lombok Strait
Flores Sea
Banda Sea
Ambon
NEW GUINEA
Arafura Sea
Dili
Timor
Koepang
Melville Island
Bathurst Island
Darwin
AUSTRALIA
Timor Sea
INDIAN OCEAN
Christmas Island
N
0
500 miles
0
500km

OPPOSITE MAP OF THE FAR EASTERN THEATER

January 7 British lose battle of Slim River; central Malaya is lost

January 11 Japanese occupy Kuala Lumpur

Japanese land at Menado, Kema, and Bangka Roads in the Celebes

January 12 Japanese occupy Tarakan, Dutch Borneo

January 24 Japanese land at Balikpapan, Dutch Borneo

Japanese occupy Kendari in the Celebes

January 25 British decide to retreat to Singapore Island

January 26 British air and naval attacks on Japanese convoy off Endau fail

January 30 Japanese seize Ambon in eastern NEI

January 31 Final British troops cross into Singapore Island

February 4 Battle of Makassar Strait; Japanese air power turns back Allied Combined Striking Force

February 8 Japanese conduct night assault across Johore Strait onto Singapore Island

February 14–17 Battle of Bangka Strait; Japanese air power again forces the Combined Striking Force to retreat

February 15 British forces on Singapore surrender

Japanese capture Bangka Island and Palembang, Sumatra

February 16 Japanese occupy Bandjermasin, Dutch Borneo

February 18 Japanese occupy Bali

February 19 Japanese carrier force conducts raid on Darwin, Australia

February 20 Japanese land on Timor Island

February 27–March 1 Naval battle of the Java Sea

March 9 NEI surrenders

ATTACKER'S CAPABILITIES

Japanese air power in 1941

The IJAAF's outstanding fighter during the campaign was the Ki-43, later given the Allied reporting name of "Oscar." Just coming into service at the start of the war, the Ki-43 equipped the 59th and 64th Sentai which were involved in operations over Malaya, Singapore, Sumatra, and Java. (Yasuho Izawa Collection)

Overall situation

The Japanese Imperial Army and Navy allocated a significant proportion of their respective air forces to the Southeast Asia campaign to create a significant numerical advantage over the combined Allied air forces. In addition, they had the massive advantage of being able to concentrate on the decisive objectives against spread-out Allied air forces which were hamstrung by a complex command structure. However, this advantage was less than it might appear since the Japanese air forces were actually two different forces – the IJAAF and the IJNAF. The IJNAF and the IJAAF fought virtually parallel air wars. These forces did cooperate, but only at the operational level. They did not conduct coordinated actions on the tactical level. The IJNAF focused on the initial effort to gain air superiority and conducted all maritime strike missions during the campaign. None of its operations were conducted in support of the ground offensive. Because of the range of its aircraft and its ability to navigate over water, the IJNAF also played the leading role in the campaign against the NEI.

The IJNAF carried the weight of the air war against China from 1937 to 1941. It conducted long-range strikes against Chinese cities and gained air superiority by attacking Chinese air bases. IJNAF fighters were able to escort the bombers and shoot down enough Chinese fighters to cripple the Chinese air force. The IJAAF lacked the modern aircraft required to conduct such a campaign. By the start of the Pacific War, the IJAAF had closed the capabilities gap with the IJNAF. But there was still no common doctrine between the two service air forces and no effort had been made to develop common operational skills. Even under wartime conditions, there was a high degree of interservice rivalry and distrust.

Imperial Japanese Navy Air Force

Organization

The IJN was unique in that it had both carrier-based and land-based units of fighters and bombers. At the start of the war, IJN land-based air units were administratively placed under the 11th Air Fleet. This was broken down into three air flotillas and 37 air groups. The three air flotillas, the 21st, 22nd, and 23rd, were allocated to support operations in Southeast Asia. Each air flotilla was composed of several air groups (*kokutai*). The IJN initially organized its air groups as mixed formations of strike aircraft and fighters so that each could conduct a variety of missions, but by the start of the war this was changed so that an air group was composed of a single type of aircraft. Tactically, the air group was divided into a squadron (*chutai*) of nine aircraft; this was composed of three sections (*shotai*) of three aircraft each.

An air group was deployed with only its flying elements since ground support elements were considered part of the base where the air unit was formed and from which it took its name. This was important since it made the air group less flexible as the flying elements and the ground crews were not always together. However, this had little effect during the relatively short period of the conquest of Malaya and the NEI. The IJNAF was able to move aircraft all over the theater to friendly bases and constantly move aircraft forward as new bases were captured. When the war began, the 21st and 23rd Air Flotillas were deployed to Formosa with the initial mission of crippling American air power in the Philippines. These formations were equipped with 90 Mitsubishi A6M "Zeros," the finest fighters in Southeast Asia. The 22nd Air Flotilla was positioned on bases near Saigon in French Indochina. This formation had the mission of protecting Japanese invasion convoys headed for southern Thailand and northern Malaya and of attacking and destroying Allied naval forces in the South China Sea. The total strength of the three air flotillas was just over 400 combat aircraft.

Doctrine and tactics

As it grew in the 1920s and 1930s, the IJNAF was focused on maritime attack. The IJN's elaborate set-piece battle plan against the United States Navy (USN) as part of its decisive battle concept had a large role for land-based air forces to play. However, when Japan invaded China in 1937, the IJN discovered that its land-based air force had strategic reach against ground targets. To gain air superiority in China, the IJNAF learned that the most effective tactic was mounting attacks by large groups of bombers escorted by large groups of fighters. This method was successful in smashing the Nationalist Chinese Air Force and was to be used against the Allies when the Pacific War opened.

Combat over China provided the IJNAF with many valuable lessons. It proved that using fighters to provide long-range escort to bombers was possible; in fact, it was proven essential if bomber losses were to be kept to sustainable levels. Tactically, there were important lessons for the fighter force. The value of individual air duels was minimized and improvements were made to discipline and to the use of the basic tactical formation, the three-fighter *shotai*. Air combat operations over China gave the Japanese their first real experience in air combat and are an overlooked reason for their initial success against the Allies.

The Mitsubishi G3M reflected the IJN's preference for a long-range bomber which it could operate from land bases throughout the Pacific. This long range proved essential during the NEI campaign. (Naval History and Heritage Command)

In the air war over China, the IJNAF also developed bad habits and took away the wrong lessons regarding modern air warfare. The tactical doctrine for escort fighters was to provide "indirect cover" for bombers. This meant that the fighters flew above and at some distance from the bombers they were tasked to protect. The reason for this was to keep the fighters free to maneuver and able to leave the formation to go chase enemy fighters when the opportunity presented itself. This tactic worked in China against the weak Chinese fighter force. Against a more skilled opponent, the tactic left the bombers unescorted and had the potential to cause heavy losses.

When IJNAF fighters engaged their counterparts, they preferred acrobatics and one-on-one dogfights. This was linked to the ancient Japanese tradition of personal combat. It also provided an opportunity for personal glory. This was true even when the fighters were assigned to bomber escort, even if it left the bombers unprotected. The most prevalent Japanese maneuver was the *hineri-komi* or "turning-in" maneuver which played to the strength of the Zero. It was developed in the mid-1930s; by executing a twisting loop followed by a diving curve, the Japanese pilot with an enemy fighter on his tail could quickly turn the tables. By the start of the Pacific War, it was a common tactic taught to all IJN fighter pilots and had even spread to the IJAAF. It was deadly against inexperienced Allied pilots. But dogfighting was not the tactic employed by Western fighter pilots, who preferred more effective high-speed hit-and-run attacks. This tactic relied on superior attitude, aircraft speed, and firepower. Against a modern opponent, the Zero's strongpoints were not superior speed or firepower, and thus Zero pilots had difficulty executing hit-and-run attacks.

The *shotai* consisted of a leader and two wingmen. In combat, these flew in a rough triangle with the two wingmen trailing the leader at a slightly higher altitude. A well-trained *shotai* could maintain formation and conduct hit-and-run tactics even while executing acrobatics.

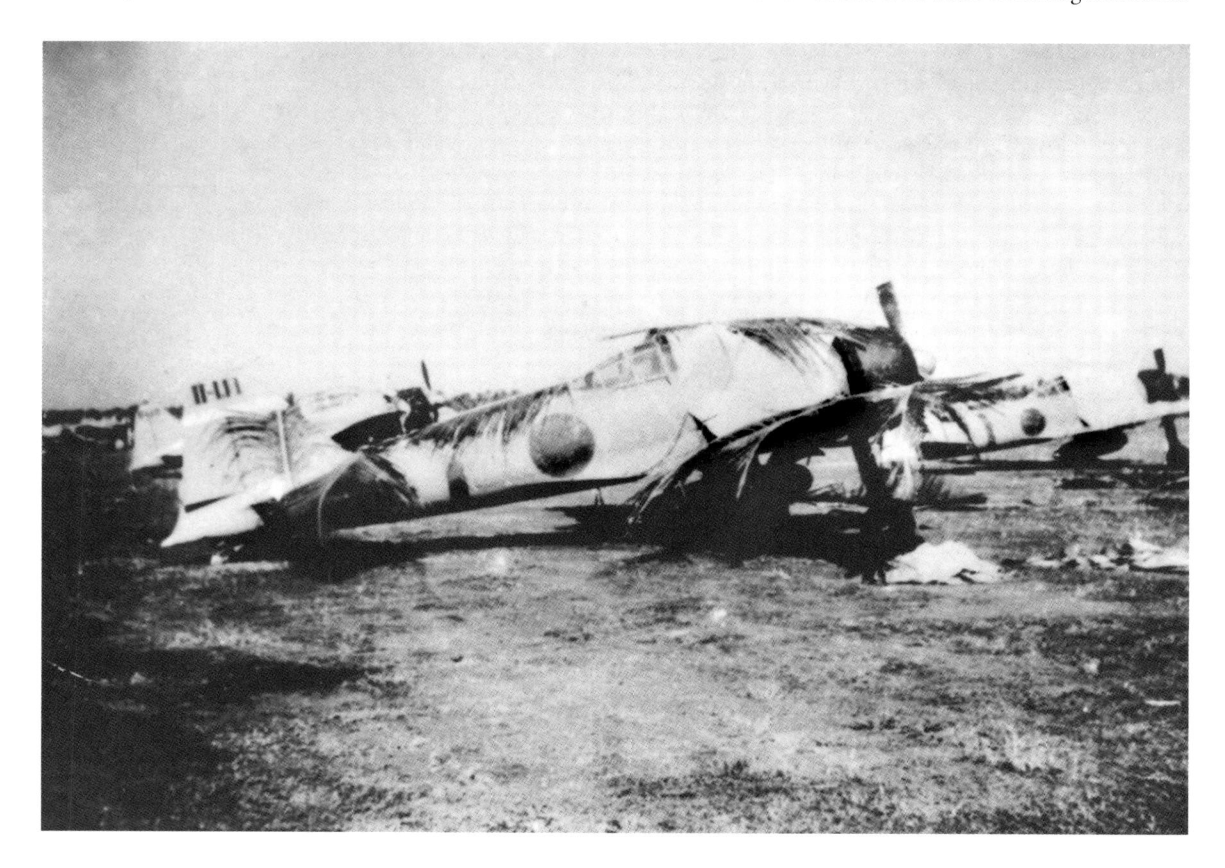

The 22nd Air Flotilla formed a unit equipped with A6M2 fighters. The formation was named after its commander, Commander Yamada Yutaka and was staffed by pulling pilots from the Tainan and 3rd Air Group. This is a Zero from the Yamada Unit at Kota Bharu which has been given a measure of camouflage against potential RAF attack. The Yamada Unit was responsible for covering 22nd Air Flotilla bomber operations over Malaya, Singapore, and western Borneo and later over Sumatra and western Java. (Australian War Memorial)

If this discipline failed, Japanese pilots reverted to their natural instinct for dogfighting. This level of discipline and cohesion was only possible after years of training and was present in the pilots of the Tainan and 3rd Air Groups. It was not present to the same degree in units of the IJAAF.

Units and aircraft

In preparation for war, the IJNAF formed a new fighter air group at Tainan on Formosa on October 1, 1941. The unit had been initially assigned 72 Mitsubishi A5M4 Type 96 Carrier Fighters and six Mitsubishi C5M2 Type 98 Reconnaissance Planes. The new Mitsubishi A6M2 Navy Carrier Fighter Type 0 soon began to replace the old A5M4s. At the start of the war, the unit had 45 A6M, 12 A5M4s, and six reconnaissance aircraft. An extensive training program was begun to prepare the Zeros for long-range missions and for coordinated operations with bombers. This unit had the critical mission of escorting bombers to hit American air bases in the Philippines. With the IJN's carriers committed to the Pearl Harbor attack, the Japanese made the gamble that aircraft flying from Formosa could neutralize American air power based in the Philippines. The A6M2, soon to be known universally as the "Zero," was a game changer and is described below. It replaced the A5M4 fighter, which was an extremely maneuverable machine but lacked the range of the Zero. The Tainan Air Group was also equipped with the Mitsubishi C5M1 for reconnaissance and as a navigation leader for the fighters, which had no radios. The Tainan Air Group began the war with a large percentage of combat veteran pilots and went on to gain a formidable reputation during the opening months of the war. It began the war by striking American air bases in the Philippines and from January 1942 led the Japanese invasion of the NEI.

The 3rd Air Group was also considered an elite formation by the Japanese. It was the first to be equipped with only fighters, breaking the previous practice of equipping an air group with different types of aircraft to conduct different missions. The unit was formed in April 1941 as a mixed unit of fighters and bombers but by September would assume its organization as a fighter-only unit. Most of the pilots in the unit were highly experienced, having seen extensive service in China. After transferring to Takao on Formosa in mid-October, the unit began intensive training for its long-range strike against American air bases in the Philippines. Achieving the highest possible fuel economy was critical since the principal American air base, Clark Field, was some 600 miles distant. At the start of the war, the unit had 45 Zeros, 12 A5M4s, and six C5M2s on hand. The Japanese effectively gained air superiority over the Philippines after only a few days. As early as January 15, the 3rd Air Group began to strike targets in the NEI. The unit played a leading role in the February 3 attack on Surabaya which gained the Japanese air superiority over eastern Java.

There were also fighters attached directly to the 22nd Air Flotilla including 25 Zeros, 12 A5M4s, and six more C5M2 reconnaissance aircraft. These aircraft were known as the Yamada Unit and were based at airfields near Saigon in southern Indochina; they constituted the only IJN fighters available for operations against Malaya and Singapore when the war opened.

The Mitsubishi A6M2 Model 21 Type 0 fighter was the best fighter in the Far East in 1941. Like most Japanese fighters, it was designed for supreme maneuverability. Added to this was an exceptional range which allowed it to strike targets throughout Southeast Asia. The fighter outperformed all opposition in China beginning in September 1940, and despite adequate reporting of the new fighter's prowess, Allied pilots in Malaya and the NEI were caught by surprise by a fighter with superior performance characteristics to those that they were flying. The top speed of the Zero was 331mph, which was superior to almost all Allied fighters, and its climbing ability was unmatched. The fighter was also fairly well armed with two 20mm cannons in the wings and two 7.7mm machine guns in the fuselage. However, the 20mm guns were slow firing and carried relatively few rounds. The Zero's primary weakness was an inability to take damage. Because making the aircraft as light as possible was required to give it great range, the Zero lacked armor or self-sealing fuel tanks. All things considered, though, when combined with an experienced pilot, the Zero was virtually unbeatable during the campaign, at least by the fighters available to the Allies.

IJNAF bomber groups

The Kanoya Air Group was formed in April 1936 at the Kanoya Air Base. It was one of the most active air groups during 1937–38 operations against China. In September 1941, it returned to Japan for conversion to the Mitsubishi G4M bomber and began intensive training on torpedo attack tactics. By the start of the war it was the IJN's best land-based maritime attack unit. In late November, half of the unit was transferred to bases near Saigon in direct response to the arrival of British battleship *Prince of Wales* in the Indian Ocean. Three of the unit's *chutai* were sent to Saigon with a reserve of nine aircraft. The other three *chutai* remained in Formosa. This unit played a key role in the destruction of the Royal Navy's Force Z on December 10. It continued active throughout the Malaya and NEI campaigns flying mainly out of Kendari in the Celebes. The unit hit targets all over the theater from Surabaya, to Darwin in Australia, to the moving Allied Combined Striking Force.

The Takao Air Group was formed in April 1938 at Takao Air Base on Formosa. The unit was initially issued with Mitsubishi G3M2 bombers and saw combat action in China during 1938 and 1940. In May 1941, the Takao Air Group was the first unit to receive the new G4M bombers. In July, the unit was transferred to bases in China to receive combat training. During these operations, the air group conducted several missions without loss. In early September, the unit returned to Takao to prepare for the start of hostilities with the Allies. At the start of the war the Takao Air Group had six *chutai* with a total of 54 bombers. The unit's initial combat operations at the start of the Pacific War were directed at American air bases in the Philippines. This strike against Clark Air Base was very successful with the loss of a single G4M1. In January, the unit was transferred to Jolo Island and on January 8 began operations against the NEI with a raid on Tarakan. Once Kendari was captured, most of the Takao Air Group was staged there. The unit took part in the first attack on Surabaya on February 3 and later sank the USN seaplane tender *Langley*.

The Genzan Air Group was formed in November 1940 in the city of Genzan (Wonsan in Korean) and initially equipped with G3M1 bombers. It gained combat experience in China before returning to Genzan in September 1941. The next month it transferred to Takao on Formosa. It entered the war with 36 G3Ms in four *chutai*. The unit took part in the attack on the Royal Navy's Force Z and continued active throughout the campaign hitting targets on Malaya, Singapore, and Sumatra.

The Mihoro Air Group was formed in October 1940 at Mihoro Air Base on Hokkaido. After brief combat action in China in 1941, it returned to Japan in August 1941 and entered the war with 36 G3M Model 21 and 22 organized into four *chutai*. It participated in the destruction of Force Z and remained active throughout the campaign.

The final bomber unit was the 1st Air Group. It was formed in April 1941 at Kanoya and initially was equipped with 36 G3Ms and 24 A5M4 fighters. After training, it was deployed to China where it gained combat experience from June to August. Following its return to Japan, it lost its fighter unit and was deployed to Formosa in mid-November as part of the 21st Air Flotilla. Its initial wartime operations were directed at American bases in the Philippines. By February 1, the 1st Air Group was deployed to Kendari and participated in attacks on eastern Java and then against Darwin on February 19. The unit was then transferred to Rabaul in the South Pacific in late February, to make up for the heavy losses suffered during an action with USN carrier *Lexington*.

The Mitsubishi G3M Navy Attack Bomber (later given the reporting name "Nell" by the Allies) was the IJN's first land-based medium bomber. Design work began in 1933 at the behest of Admiral Yamamoto Isoroku who was head of the Technical Division of the Naval

Before the war, the Kanoya and Takao Air Groups received the new Mitsubishi G4M1 bomber like those pictured here. The G4M1 Model 11 was the version in service in December 1941. It possessed a top speed of 266mph. Defensive armament consisted of a tail-mounted 20mm gun and four flexible machine guns. The aircraft's bomb load was identical to the G3M but range was increased to 3,256nm. Despite real weaknesses, the G4M was the outstanding bomber of the Malaya and NEI campaigns. (Yasuho Izawa Collection)

Bureau of Aeronautics. Yamamoto foresaw the need for a long-range bomber to support the IJN's attritional strategy against the USN as it steamed into the Central Pacific. The G3M was put into production in mid-1936 and proved extremely successful since it could carry a 1,760lb torpedo or a similar bomb load for 2,365nm. This aircraft set the pattern for IJNAF designs, with long range at the expense of protection. At the start of the Pacific War, it was the most numerous IJN land-based bomber though it was in the process of being replaced by the G4M. It is scarcely remembered that this forgotten aircraft was a principal agent in the destruction of British battleship *Prince of Wales* in December 1941. Though the G3M had conducted long-range strikes against targets in China since August 1937, the Royal Navy had no idea that the IJN possessed an aircraft which could deliver effective torpedo attacks at long range.

The other outstanding land-based IJN bomber of the early war period was the Mitsubishi G4M1 Navy Type 1 Attack Bomber Model 11. The aircraft was replacing the G3M medium bomber and was destined to remain in production for the remainder of the war. Later in the war, it was given the reporting name of "Betty" by the Allies. The G4M was designed as a long-range maritime strike aircraft which could carry one 1,760lb torpedo or a similar payload of bombs. The aircraft's range – 3,256nm – was astounding for a medium bomber, which made it ideally suited for supporting the Japanese advance through Southeast Asia. The bomber was also fairly fast at 266mph and it carried a powerful self-protection suite of four 7.7mm machine guns and a 20mm cannon in its tail. The G4M was a superb offensive platform. However, as was the case with the Zero, the performance of the IJN's newest bomber was achieved by making the aircraft as light as possible. This meant that there was no armor protection for the crew and that the 1,294 gallons of fuel in the wing were carried in tanks that were not self-sealing. The G4M had obvious vulnerabilities if the Allies could exploit them.

The Mitsubishi C5M2 was designed as a fast reconnaissance aircraft. With a top speed of 303mph, it could evade most Allied fighters of the period. The IJN version was the Type 98 Reconnaissance Plane Model 1 C5M2 which had naval radios and camera equipment. The C5M2 was often used as a navigational guide aircraft for single-engine fighters. Like all other Japanese aircraft, its high performance was gained at the cost of no armor and no self-sealing fuel tanks.

The Mitsubishi G3M was the mainstay bomber of the IJNAF during the early period of the war. It entered widespread service in 1936. At the start of the war, the most numerous version was the G3M2 Model 22 with a top speed of 232mph and a defensive suite of one 20mm cannon in a dorsal turret and four 7.7mm machine guns in flexible mounts, including in a retractable dorsal turret as can be seen in this view. The aircraft's range was outstanding, but its bomb load was mediocre for a medium bomber. (Philip Jarrett Collection)

Seaplane carriers and tenders

Since the IJN's fleet carriers were all assigned to the Pearl Harbor operation, there were few carriers left for the advance into Southeast Asia. Only the light carrier *Ryujo* was assigned to the Southern Operation (the Japanese name for the Southeast Asia offensive). It was an unsuccessful ship launched in 1931 and rebuilt twice before the war to correct design defects. *Ryujo* had a nominal aircraft capacity of 48 but only embarked 26 (with another eight reserve aircraft) for operations in Southeast Asia. Included in its air group was a fighter unit of 12 A5M4s and 14 Nakajima Type 97 B5N1/2 "Kate" attack planes. Because of the small size of *Ryujo*'s flight deck, only six Kates could be spotted for a single launch, which dramatically restricted its effectiveness. Though the B5N could carry both bombs and torpedoes, only bombs were used in the NEI campaign owing to torpedo shortages and maintenance issues.

An overlooked aspect of the IJN's plan to cover the invasion convoys in Malaya and the NEI was the large-scale use of seaplane carriers and tenders. These were extremely useful since they carried a relatively large number of floatplanes. The aircraft were launched from catapults mounted on the ships and recovered alongside in the water and were hoisted back aboard using cranes. Purpose-built seaplane carriers *Chitose* and *Mizuho* each had a capacity of 24 seaplanes. Augmenting these were a number of seaplane tenders which were conversions of large and fairly fast merchant ships in the immediate period before the war. Four seaplane tenders were allocated to support the advance into Southeast Asia, including *Kamikawa Maru*, which embarked 14 seaplanes, and *Sagara Maru*, *Sanuki Maru*, and *Sanyo Maru*, each of which embarked eight. The most common seaplanes were the Mitsubishi F1M2 Type 0 Observation Plane, which was a two-place biplane with a top speed of 230mph. The aircraft was designed as a short-range observation plane, but its extreme maneuverability, three 7.7mm machine guns, and ability to carry a small bomb load made it suitable for a number of roles including fighter, dive-bomber, and convoy escort aircraft. The other aircraft typically embarked was the Aichi E13A1 Type 0 Reconnaissance Seaplane. This was a three-seat, single-engine floatplane with a top speed of 234mph. It proved outstanding in a general patrol and reconnaissance role since it had an endurance of 15 hours and a range of over 1,100nm.

The carrier Striking Force

The *Kido Butai* (usually rendered as Striking Force) was the IJN's carrier force. It was composed of three carrier divisions, each with two carriers, and a heavy escort of two fast battleships, two heavy cruisers, and a flotilla of destroyers led by a light cruiser. Since each of the six carriers carried three squadrons, this was a formidable collection of naval air power with over 400 aircraft. The embarked air group included a fighter unit with the Zero, a dive-bomber squadron with the Aichi D3A1 Type 99 Carrier Bomber, and a squadron of attack planes with the Nakajima B5N2 Type 97 Carrier Attack Aircraft. These squadrons were given the cream of Japanese naval aviation, which made the *Kido Butai* the most powerful naval force on the planet with its ability to bring overwhelming numbers of excellent aircraft crewed by the highest-quality pilots against a single target. Though allocated against Pearl Harbor, the commander of the Combined Fleet Admiral Yamamoto planned to bring the *Kido Butai* into Southeast Asia to support the final stages of the NEI campaign. It made its first appearance during the campaign on January 14 and, on February 19, conducted a shattering strike on Darwin with four carriers launching 188 aircraft. From there, it moved to a position south of Java to catch Allied shipping attempting to flee the NEI. Its only strike on Java was against the port of Tjilatjap on March 5 with 180 aircraft. The *Kido Butai* could have been more involved against Java had Japanese land-based aircraft not secured air superiority.

Imperial Japanese Army Air Force

The IJAAF was composed of several air armies (*kokugun*). Each air army was composed of as many as three air divisions (*hikoshidan*); each of these was typically composed of three air brigades (*hikodan*). This formation controlled a number of regiments (*sentai*) and independent squadrons (*chutai*). An IJAAF air brigade was roughly similar in size to an RAF Wing. Each brigade typically consisted of three *sentai*. The *sentai* was the building block for IJAAF operations and was capable of independent operations. A *sentai* was similar in size to a USAAF group. It usually consisted of three *chutai* and a headquarters flight. There were also independent squadrons, most often composed of reconnaissance aircraft. A *hikotai* was formed to control several independent squadrons.

The IJAAF formation assigned to support the 25th Army in Malaya and the 15th Army in Burma was the 3rd Air Division. Commanded by Lieutenant General Sugawara Michioho, it was a large formation with four subordinate air brigades, 14 *sentai*, an independent *chutai*, and two *hikotai* controlling five more independent *chutai*. Total combat aircraft assigned came to just under 500. These were broken down into 189 fighters, 269 bombers of all types, and 35 reconnaissance aircraft. Of these, the 10th Air Brigade with 81 aircraft was slated to support operations in Burma with a *sentai* of fighters, a *sentai* of light bombers, and a *sentai* of heavy bombers.

IJAAF doctrine

The IJAAF subscribed to the classic notion of what is now known as offensive counterair operations. In IJAAF parlance this was called "aerial exterminating action." This called for the destruction of enemy aircraft on the ground if possible by intensive and sustained attacks by bombers and fighters, and the destruction of enemy aircraft in the air by fighters. Once air superiority was gained, the IJAAF could turn its attention to ground support for the army. There was friction between the 3rd Air Division and the 25th Army throughout the campaign since the latter did not think that the air force was devoting enough of its efforts to ground support. In fact, the latest doctrinal guidance issued in 1940 and called *Air Operations*

The IJAAF's preference for dogfighting was epitomized by the Ki-27. It was a superlative dogfighter but was not well suited for delivering slashing attacks from higher altitudes, which became the preferred tactic of Western air forces. Note the fixed undercarriage, which gave it an outdated appearance. (Netherlands Institute for Military History)

Essentials stated that there should be a balance between the "aerial exterminating action" and ground support operations. During the campaign, the 3rd Air Division acted more as an independent air arm than as an extension of the ground forces. The 3rd Air Division continued to emphasize counterair operations during the campaign even after it was apparent that the RAF posed little threat.

IJAAF units and aircraft

The IJAAF allocated five fighter *sentai* to support the Malayan campaign. Of these, three were still equipped with the older Nakajima Ki-27 (later given the Allied reporting name "Nate") and two had received the Nakajima Ki-43 (Allied reporting name "Oscar"). The Ki-27 units were the 1st, 11th, and 77th Sentai. The 1st Sentai dated from 1915 and was the first aviation unit of the Japanese Army. It was a veteran unit which had seen combat against Soviet forces during the Nomonhan Conflict from June to September 1939. The 11th Sentai traced its origins to 1932 and had also been blooded at Nomonhan. The 77th Sentai was formed in July 1937 and had extensive combat experience in China. It was withdrawn from Malaya and sent to support the attack into Burma in the second part of December; the unit's 3rd Chutai returned to Malaya on January 8.

The 59th and 64th Sentai received the new Ki-43 before the opening of the Pacific War. These were the first IJAAF units to receive the new fighter. The 59th Sentai was formed in July 1938 and received the Ki-43 in June 1941. The unit had gained combat experience in China. The 64th Sentai received its first Ki-43s in September. The unit also had extensive combat experience against both the Russians and Chinese.

The backbone of the IJA's fighter force during the campaign was the Nakajima Ki-27. This aircraft entered service in 1937 but by late 1941 was nearing obsolescence. It looked antiquated with its fixed undercarriage. However, flown by an experienced pilot it could still defeat Allied fighters of the period. The Ki-27 had a top speed of 292mph, which made it somewhat slower than most Allied fighters. It did possess superior maneuverability, which reflected the preferred IJAAF tactic of engaging in turning dogfights. The aircraft was under-armed with only two 7.7mm machine guns.

The Ki-27 was replaced by the Ki-43. The aircraft was just entering service at the start of the war after a series of developmental problems and made its combat debut over Malaya. Since it did not have the same superior maneuverability as the Ki-27, it took the IJAAF a while to warm to the new aircraft. It did possess a retractable undercarriage and was faster at 308mph and had greater range. The Ki-43 carried the same inadequate armament as the Ki-27 of only two 7.7mm machine guns and had no protection for the pilot or fuel tanks. The big improvement offered by the Ki-43 was its greater operational radius of 330–360nm; this was much better than the Ki-27 which had an operational radius of only 240nm. The greater radius was mandatory if the IJAAF wanted to carry out its doctrine of gaining air superiority in the Pacific War since the distance to enemy bases in Southeast Asia was so great. Its appearance was similar to the A6M Zero fighter and Allied pilots had difficulty telling the two aircraft apart since they were unaware that the IJAAF had placed a new fighter in service. In spite of its shortcomings, it was a formidable opponent when in the hands of experienced pilots.

The bombers of the 3rd Air Division included a mix of heavy, light, and army cooperation aircraft. All were as good as or better than their Allied counterparts.

The standard IJAAF heavy bomber was the Mitsubishi Ki-21 Army Type 97 Heavy Bomber Model 1 (later given the Allied reporting name of "Sally"). This was a two-engine aircraft which would have been considered a medium bomber by the Allies. The IJAAF did not possess a true heavy bomber like the American B-17. The Ki-21 first reached service in August 1938 when the 60th Sentai took delivery of the first aircraft. The new bomber was successful in combat operations over China. By the start of the Pacific War, the latest version was the Ki-21-IIa which possessed greater speed and ceiling than earlier versions. Even with these improvements, the aircraft was already approaching obsolescence. Performance was mediocre with a top speed of some 302mph and its normal payload was 1,653lb. Protection was an issue since the aircraft lacked armor and self-sealing fuel tanks and it carried only five small-caliber (7.7mm) machine guns for self-defense. It was well-liked by its crews since it was easy to fly and maintain.

The 3rd Air Division was assigned four heavy bomber *sentai* – the 12th, 60th, 62nd, and 98th. The 12th Sentai had seen action over China and against the Russians at Nomonhan but did not receive its Ki-21s until 1940. The 60th Sentai was one of the first units to get the Ki-21 and had brief combat experience against the Chinese. The 62nd Sentai was formed in October 1941, fought briefly over Malaya, losing 12 bombers, and then went to Burma. The 98th Sentai was formed in 1938 and received its Ki-21s in late 1939. Over 120 Ki-21s were available at the start of the campaign.

The standard IJAAF light bomber was the Kawasaki Ki-48 Army Type 99 Twin-engine Light Bomber Model 1. Two *sentai*, the 75th and 90th, flew this aircraft during the campaign. The 75th Sentai had combat experience over China but did not receive its

This photograph shows a Ki-21-Ib of the 60th Sentai, 3rd Chutai. The IJAAF called the Ki-21 a heavy bomber, but it was a medium bomber by any measure and clearly a mediocre one at that. In addition to a very weak defensive armament and a lack of armor and self-sealing fuel tanks, it possessed an unimpressive normal range of some 932 miles. (Philip Jarrett Collection)

Ki-48s until right before the war. The 90th Sentai also had combat experience, and in July 1941 began to receive the Ki-48 to replace the Ki-30. The version in service at the start of the war was the Ki-48-I. Like the Ki-21, it performed well over China but was vulnerable against modern opponents. Its top speed (298mph) was insufficient to avoid interception, it lacked protection for its four-man crew and its fuel tanks, and its defensive armament consisted of only three 7.7mm machine guns. Its maximum bomb load was a paltry 882lb.

The Mitsubishi Ki-30 Type 97 Light Bomber entered service with the IJAAF in 1938. The aircraft was easy to fly and maintain, but at the start of the war was obsolescent and unable to operate in contested airspace. Given the Allied reporting name of "Ann," the Ki-30 was a single-engine, two-place aircraft with unimpressive characteristics. Its top speed was only 263mph and it had a maximum bomb load of only 882lb. If caught by enemy fighters it was extremely vulnerable since it had no armor or self-sealing fuel tanks and its defensive armament consisted of only one wing-mounted 7.7mm machine gun with another 7.7mm gun firing aft. The 27th and 31st Sentai flew this aircraft and both had gained combat experience over China.

Reconnaissance was performed by a number of different types including the Ki-51, Ki-46, Ki-15, and Ki-36. The Ki-51 was an improved version of the Ki-30 which was also used for ground attack. It was better protected and more maneuverable and liked by its crews. The Mitsubishi Ki-15 Army Type 97 Command Reconnaissance Plane Model 2 was a fast single-engine, two-man aircraft capable of high-altitude operations. It was the army version of the IJNAAF's C5M2. It was being replaced by the Ki-46. The Mitsubishi Ki-46 Type 100 Command Reconnaissance Plane Model 2 was the outstanding aircraft of the lot and one of the best reconnaissance aircraft of the entire war. The Ki-46-II available at the beginning of the war was fitted with two powerful 1,050hp engines, which gave it a maximum speed of 375mph. Service ceiling was just over 35,000ft; its combination of high speed and high altitude made it largely impervious to Allied fighters in Southeast Asia. It was deployed in small detachments to perform high-altitude reconnaissance all over the theater.

Under the command of the IJA's Southern Army were several units of transport aircraft equipped with the Mitsubishi Ki-57 and the Nakajima Ki-34. The former was the transport version of the Ki-21 and the latter was a medium-range civilian airliner design. These were important assets for helping IJAAF units stage to new bases and were used in the airborne attack on Palembang in February 1942.

The fact that a light bomber with a top speed under 300mph, a defensive suite of only three machine guns, no armor or self-sealing fuel tanks, and a payload of 882lb could have any success at all demonstrates the weakness of Allied air defenses during the campaign. This is the IJAAF's most numerous light bomber of the campaign, the Kawasaki Ki-48. (Philip Jarrett Collection)

DEFENDER'S CAPABILITIES

The Allies in East Asia

The RAF in Malaya

Overall situation

With the war raging in northwest Europe and the Mediterranean, RAF forces in the Far East were a low priority. But the aggressive moves by Japan underlined the reality that Great Britain would have to prepare for the probability of a war in Asia. In 1940, it was decided that the RAF in the Far East should be built up to a level of at least 366 modern aircraft, far fewer than the 566 aircraft recommended by RAF officers in the Far East. By the outbreak of hostilities with Japan, the British had failed to meet either of these figures. The Far East air commander, Air Vice-Marshal Conway Pulford, had only 158 aircraft available and most of these were not front-line aircraft. The RAF Far East Command consisted of nine RAF, five Royal Australian Air Force (RAAF), and two Royal New Zealand Air Force (RNZAF) squadrons.

The Consolidated Catalina flying boat was a successful design with an impressive range, and good defensive armament and payload. Here, two Catalinas of 205 Squadron based in Singapore are photographed on a training mission before the war. The Catalina gave outstanding service as a long-range patrol aircraft. (Library of Congress)

Command structure

In late 1940, the position of Commander-in-Chief Far East was created. Air Chief Marshal Sir Robert Brooke-Popham was appointed as the first officer to hold this post and he had his headquarters in Singapore up and running on November 14. The new Air Officer Commanding Far East Command, replacing Brooke-Popham, was Pulford. He was responsible for the operations of all air units in Malaya and Singapore. In July 1941, Group Captain E. B. Rice was appointed as the first Fighter Defence Commander of Singapore and Coordinator of Air Defences of Malaya. The British Army remained responsible for antiaircraft defenses in both Malaya and Singapore.

Command arrangements following the creation of Brooke-Popham's new post remained awkward. Though he was responsible for coordinating defense planning, training, and operations of ground and air forces in Malaya, Singapore, Burma, British Borneo, and Hong Kong, his authority was limited. He did not even have full control over Army and RAF units in his area of responsibility since they continued to report

A Dutch Glenn Martin bomber crew is greeted by Pulford after arriving on Singapore Island. The British convinced the Dutch that Singapore was critical for the defense of the NEI. This prompted the Dutch to augment the defense of Singapore with several fighter and bomber squadrons before and during the campaign. (Netherlands Institute for Military History)

to their respective service chains of command. Royal Navy units in the region reported directly to London, and the governors and civil servants in the colonies reported directly to ministers in London. Thrust into an impossible situation, Brooke-Popham was in over his head. He had a headquarters staff of seven, which was clearly inadequate for the many tasks he was given. In the year following his appointment up until the start of the Pacific War, he had only limited success in reinforcing the garrisons in the Far East or in harmonizing the defense planning among the many entities under his nominal control. It had been agreed that Brooke-Popham would be replaced on November 1, 1941, but with war looming with the Japanese this did not occur. After the conflict began, Brooke-Popham appeared unable to provide the required leadership so London arranged for him to hand over his command to Lieutenant General Sir Henry Pownall on December 27.

Air bases and air base defense

In July 1940, the Chiefs of Staff in London authorized an expansion of the air forces stationed in Malaya and Singapore. To house the envisioned 366 aircraft, the RAF surveyed the colonies with an eye to extending the reconnaissance and bombing reach from new airfields. During this process, the RAF failed to consult with the Army on how the new airfields would be defended. Since the Army was responsible for the ground and antiaircraft defenses of the airfields, this was a major omission and another indication of the shambolic state of British defense planning in the period leading up to hostilities with Japan. The RAF wished to place the new airfields as far forward as possible in order to interdict an invading force long before it could reach Malaya. This meant that many of the new airfields were placed in northern Malaya and along the eastern coast. The limited number of British ground forces precluded a strong defense of all these facilities. The result was that the British built new facilities which were easily captured and used by the Japanese. The placement of the new airfields also meant they were within easy range of Japanese airfields after the Japanese acquired air bases in southern Indochina.

Singapore shown burning after a Japanese air attack. The four airfields and the naval base on the island were the primary Japanese targets on the island, but often the Japanese struck the city itself causing heavy casualties. British air defenses protecting the city and the nearby military targets were almost totally ineffective during the campaign. (Library of Congress)

The new base construction program was ambitious; in fact, it was so comprehensive that it was simply beyond the capabilities of the available contractors to execute. Labor, construction materials, and equipment were all in short supply, so the targeted completion date of the end of 1941 was not met. Little work was done on building dispersal areas and the earth revetments in place were inadequate to provide blast protection for parked aircraft. There was no use of camouflage, making the aircraft stationed there easy targets. Few of the airfields had surfaced runways. Most were grass strips that became quagmires during monsoon season, which hindered maintenance and repair.

The expansion program focused on upgrading seven existing facilities and building 16 new ones. By the start of the war, there was still much work left undone.

Condition of RAF Bases December 8, 1941			
Malaya			
Base	Antiaircraft Guns	Dispersal Areas	Runway Surface
Alor Star	4 x 3in	Complete	Hard
Butterworth	None	Not complete	Hard, being extended
Jabi	None	None	Graded, not surfaced
Lubok Kiap	None	None	Partly surfaced
Penang	None	None	Grass
Sungei Patani	7 x 3.7in	Almost complete	Grass
Gong Kedah	3 x 3in	Almost complete	Hard
Kota Bharu	4 x 3in	Almost complete	Grass
Machang	None	None	Hard
Kuantan	None	Complete	Grass
Ipoh	None	None	Grass/hard
Kuala Lumpur	None	None	Grass
Kluang	None	Complete	Grass, hard surface under construction
Kahang	None	Complete	Grass
Singapore Island			
Kallang	Note 1	Complete	Grass
Seletar	Note 1, 8 x 40mm	Complete	Grass
Sembawang	Note 1	Complete	Grass
Tengah	Note 1	Partly complete	Grass and concrete
Note 1: Airfield protection provided by Singapore City and Naval Base antiaircraft guns			

Air warning system

When the expansion of facilities began in July 1940, the air defense system had to be built from scratch. This work was scheduled to be completed by the end of 1941, but as in the case of airfield construction, it proved impossible to meet this timeline. An effective air defense system required modern aircraft, radar, and other warning equipment, solid communications, antiaircraft guns, and above all trained personnel. All of these were either non-existent or in short supply when the war began.

Warning of Japanese air attack was totally inadequate. While 20 radar installations were planned, only six were in place at the start of the war. These were all on or near Singapore. Four were positioned on Singapore Island to give a 130-mile warning of aircraft approaching from sea. The other two were placed on the southeast and southwest tip of Johore. In addition to radar, the RAF set up an Observation Corps based on the one in the United Kingdom. The civilian volunteers were poorly organized and lacked proper training, equipment, and communications. The mountainous jungle terrain in central Malaya prevented the placement of any observation posts in those areas. The observers reported to the two control rooms at Singapore and Kuala Lumpur. These rooms were linked with the Dutch observer system in the NEI. Despite the elaborate plans, the net result was huge gaps in coverage which were never closed during the campaign. When the war began, the fighter control center at Singapore was just becoming operational.

Antiaircraft units

Antiaircraft guns were in short supply in Malaya in December 1941. Based on experience from the Battle of Britain, the chief antiaircraft officer in Malaya believed that the minimum defense for an airfield was eight heavy (3.7in) and 16 light (40mm Bofors) guns. Brooke-Popham was promised eight heavy and eight light antiaircraft weapons for each airfield, but as seen by the preceding table, even this reduced number was not achieved and most air bases were undefended. The exceptions were the four airfields on Singapore, which were defended by the concentration of antiaircraft guns on the island positioned to protect the air bases, the naval base, and the city of Singapore. The 3.7in and 40mm Bofors guns were modern weapons, but a third of the guns actually available were 3in weapons, which

Allied airfield defenses throughout the theater were weak, and Dutch airfield defenses were the weakest. Here is a 105mm antiaircraft gun of which only four were available for the entire NEI. (Netherlands Institute for Military History)

This photograph shows RAF and Dutch aircrew in conference next to a Hudson bomber. Most RAF and Dutch bomber crews had neither operational nor combat experience before the war. Many Allied aircrew were fresh out of flight training at the start of the war. (Library of Congress)

was a design from World War I. Height-finding and fire-control equipment was in short supply and when available depended on manual inputs.

Training was restricted by the lack of targets and target-towing aircraft. The problems with early warning were compounded for antiaircraft crews since frequent overcast made spotting aircraft from the ground difficult. Few searchlights were available and those that were, were retained on Singapore. Coordination with friendly fighters was non-existent since there was no experience or training in this area. This problem was so acute that when the first Japanese raid against Singapore occurred on the night of December 8, no fighters were allowed to take off. While the air defense system on Singapore was the most developed, even here it proved difficult to defend the island from Japanese bombing attacks. Japanese bombers typically approached at 24,000ft. RAF fighters rarely had adequate time to make intercepts because of the incomplete radar coverage and the 35 minutes needed to climb that high. The 40mm Bofors guns were only effective against low-flying aircraft and the 30 3in guns could not engage targets at that altitude. Only the 50 radar-controlled 3.7in guns on the island could engage targets at that height.

Fighter squadrons

The RAF in the Far East was composed almost entirely of obsolescent aircraft. With the demands of the war in Europe and North Africa, and the start of Lend Lease shipments to the USSR, few aircraft were available to reinforce the Far East. Those that were shipped east were with few exceptions second rate. The RAF did stand up a number of new squadrons in Singapore in the year preceding the start of the war, and in the six months before the start of the war in December 1941, the number of aircrew assigned to the RAF Far East Command doubled. A few combat veterans of the fighting in Europe were assigned to the new squadrons, but most of the new personnel came directly from training units. The overall lack of aircrew experience in the Far East was illustrated by the high accident rate between January and September 1941. There were 67 accidents, which accounted for 22 aircraft destroyed and another 31 seriously damaged. Forty-eight aircrew were killed.

The standard fighter for the squadrons of the Far East air command was the American-produced Brewster Buffalo. This aircraft was selected not for its capabilities but because of its availability. When war broke out there were four Buffalo squadrons in the Far East including 243 RAF, 21 and 453 RAAF, and 488 (NZ) RAF Squadrons. These squadrons possessed 118 mostly inexperienced aircrew. Of these, 28 were killed or captured during the campaign.

The state of 488 (NZ) Squadron, RAF, can be taken as typical. First formed in Wellington in September 1941, on September 11 the squadron left by ship for Singapore where it arrived on October 11 after a stop in Australia. The squadron was officially designated the following day. The new unit was sent to Kallang Airfield on Singapore where it was based for the duration of the campaign. The squadron commanding officer, Squadron Leader Wilf Clouston, was a good choice to stand up the first New Zealand fighter squadron. He was born in New Zealand and had been flying with the RAF since 1936. After arriving in Singapore, the aircrews were sent to Kluang in Malaya for conversion training on the Brewster Buffalo. None of the pilots, aside from Clouston and his two flight leaders, had any experience. The 21 Buffalos were actually hand-me-downs from 67 Squadron when it left for Burma; exactly zero were operational. There were also no tools or spare parts. The New Zealanders pilfered enough spare parts from 243 Squadron and a Dutch squadron at Kallang which also flew the Buffalo to get most of their aircraft operational. During its efforts to reach an operational status, 488 Squadron lost 12 aircraft and two pilots before going into action. The aircraft carried no radios and had to rely on hand signals to communicate once in the air. Training was inhibited by the lackadaisical work schedule established by the British. Hours were restricted to 0730–1230 with most afternoons off. Wednesday was set as a half-day holiday and no work was permitted on Sunday.

On the first occasion when Buffalos from 488 Squadron met the Japanese, the result was predictable. On January 12, eight Buffalos took off to intercept a raid of 27 bombers escorted by fighters. Before they could reach the altitude of the bombers, they were attacked by Zeros with a height advantage. The Buffalos were forced to disengage; two were shot down and the others damaged for no Japanese losses. A second flight of six Buffalos took off 30 minutes later but only one made contact with the Japanese and the pilot broke off the action in order to survive. The next day, five damaged aircraft were written off. These first engagements confirmed the squadron's assessment that the Buffalo was outmatched by the Japanese. By January 24, 488 was down to its last three Buffalos. It was re-equipped with nine Hurricane fighters. After the ground crews got the nine Hurricanes ready by working impossible hours, the Japanese showed up with 27 bombers on the morning of January 27. The bombers dropped their payloads on Kallang; they destroyed two of the fighters and badly damaged the other seven.

The Brewster Buffalo was originally designed for use on USN carriers. At the start of the European War, several nations raced to place orders with Brewster for the Buffalo, which was considered in excess of USN requirements after the Grumman Wildcat had been selected as the standard carrier fighter leading up to the war. The Model 339E was the variant sold overseas. The Finns received some and the British ordered 170. The Dutch ordered the Model 339C and 339D, which were lighter and had a more powerful engine.

As a fighter, the Buffalo was a disaster. The British recognized this early on and decided the aircraft was not suitable for employment in Europe. However, against a second-rate opponent like the Japanese, the Buffalo was deemed suitable enough. The Buffalo's problem was its lack of speed and maneuverability, both not good problems to have in a fighter. The British added more weight to their Buffalos, reducing their top speed to 204mph and the rate of climb to 2,600ft per minute. The aircraft could not operate over 25,000ft and it took a painful 35 minutes to get to that altitude.

Initially, the Buffalo was heavily armed with four .50-caliber machine guns. In order to reduce the weight of the aircraft to increase its performance, the RAF replaced the .50-caliber weapons with lighter .303 machine guns and the amount of ammunition was reduced. The fuel load was also reduced. These modifications created new problems as pilots faced persistent issues with running out of ammunition or fuel.

In addition to the Buffalos, 27 Squadron was equipped with Bristol Blenheim IF night fighters. These differed from the light bomber version by carrying a gun pack under the fuselage with four .303in machine guns. Since the aircraft did not carry air intercept radars, they were of marginal use in their intended role as night fighters.

The Dutch version of the Buffalo was the B-339C and 339D models, the former with rebuilt Wright G-105 engines supplied by the Dutch and the latter with new 1,200hp Wright R-1820-40 engines. At the outbreak of war, 71 Buffalos were in the NEI. The Dutch aircraft were lighter than the version used by the RAF so had better performance. The Dutch further improved performance by halving the aircraft's fuel and ammunition loads. The Dutch Buffalo force fought to near extinction; only four remained on March 7. Thirty were destroyed in the air, 15 on the ground, and several to operational causes. (Netherlands Institute for Military History)

Fighter reinforcements arrived in limited numbers. 232 Squadron arrived by ship on January 13 with 24 pilots and 51 Hurricane II fighters in crates. Of the 24 pilots, only six were originally assigned to 232 Squadron; the others had been detached from 17, 135, and 136 Squadrons so that 232 Squadron could be sent to Singapore as quickly as possible.

The balance of 232 Squadron and another reinforcing squadron, 258 Squadron, were embarked on carrier *Formidable* when it departed Port Sudan on January 9 with 48 pilots and an identical number of Hurricane II fighters. On January 28 and 29, they were flown to Kemajoran Airfield on Java. One was lost to mechanical problems during the flight. From there they went to Sumatra and then on to Singapore. In the case of both Hurricane squadrons, the majority of the pilots were totally inexperienced in combat operations having just come from training units. Only the squadron commanders and the flight commanders had any operational experience.

After the fall of Singapore, the two Hurricane squadrons returned to Sumatra. Operations there were very difficult since the ground crews lacked the correct tools for servicing Hurricanes and spare parts were virtually non-existent. Ammunition supplies were also low. The ground crews actually came from Buffalo squadrons. All of these issues made for a very low serviceability rate.

The Hawker Hurricane was a great improvement over the Buffalo. It was a single-seat monoplane fighter which first entered RAF operational service in 1937. By 1941, the design was showing its age but it was still able to hold its own against more modern fighters. The Hurricane II was heavily armed with up to 12 wing-mounted .303in machine guns and was capable of a top speed of 318mph.

The first 51 Hurricane IIBs arrived in crates on January 13, 1942. The arrival of the Hurricane gave the RAF a fighter roughly equal in capabilities to the main Japanese fighters. This is a Hurricane IIB assigned to 488 Squadron at Kallang Airfield on January 24, 1942. (Andrew Thomas Collection)

Bomber squadrons

The most numerous bomber in the Far East was the Bristol Blenheim with three squadrons operating the aircraft. 34 Squadron was assigned 16 Blenheim IV aircraft while 62 Squadron had 11 Blenheim Is. There was also a detachment from 60 Squadron with eight Blenheim Is which was caught in Malaya on bombing practice when the war began. The detachment was returned to Burma by sea in mid-December leaving its surviving Blenheims behind. Altogether, RAF Far East Command had 47 operational Blenheims (including those of 27 Squadron) with another 15 in reserve.

The Blenheim was another example of the RAF shipping obsolescent aircraft to the Far East. When it was first delivered, it was the RAF's fastest bomber. The two 840hp Bristol Mercury VIII radial engines could propel the light bomber at speeds greater than many fighters of the period. By late 1941, however, this speed was insufficient to protect it against fighter interception. The Blenheim was extremely vulnerable to interception since it had

The most numerous RAF bomber in Malaya was the Blenheim; it equipped three squadrons and a detachment from a squadron which was present in Malaya on a training deployment when the war began. This is a Blenheim I of 62 Squadron on a prewar training mission. The Blenheim I was obsolescent with a mediocre top speed, a weak bomb load, and only two defensive machine guns. In daylight missions over contested airspace, it suffered heavily against Japanese fighters. (Andrew Thomas Collection)

an almost complete lack of armor protection and an inadequate defensive armament (only a single forward-firing machine gun and a machine gun in a dorsal turret). The aircraft's offensive potential was also limited by a typical bomb load of only two 250lb bombs. The Blenheim IV featured a redesigned nose, more powerful engines, additional armor, and a total of five machine guns, but was still limited to a top speed of only 266mph.

The standard bomber for the RAAF was the Hudson which equipped both RAAF squadrons in Malaya at the start of the war. This is a Hudson II assigned to 8 Squadron RAAF. Note that the newly arrived aircraft has not been fitted with its dorsal turret. (Andrew Thomas Collection)

The other bomber used by the RAF in the Far East was the Lockheed Hudson. Originally designed as a twin-engine civil transport, it was quickly adapted for military use and sold to the British in 1938. Both the Hudson I and II versions were deployed to the Far East. Its maximum speed was 261mph and it had the ability to carry a bomb load of 1,000lb.

The only torpedo bomber in the Far East was the ancient Vickers Vildebeest. It was a three-seat biplane which first flew in 1928 and entered RAF service in 1931. The fact that they were still in service in 1941 shows the strain the RAF was under to meet its many commitments. By 1941, the Vildebeest was obsolescent as demonstrated by its top speed of 143mph. The aircraft could carry an 18in torpedo. At the start of the war, 36 and 100 Squadrons were equipped with a total of 29 Vildebeests with another 12 in reserve. In spite of its obvious limitations, the Vildebeest fought throughout the campaign with the last surviving aircraft moving to Java on January 31. On March 6, the last two aircraft attempted to fly to Burma but crashed on Sumatra. None survived the campaign.

An important mission for the RAF Far East Command was maritime surveillance. This mission was often assigned to Hudsons and, to a lesser degree, Blenheims. For long-range reconnaissance, 205 Squadron flew the Consolidated Catalina flying boat. The Catalina was a very successful design with a long range. It was slow (179mph cruising speed), however, and thus vulnerable to interception.

The Dutch forces

The Royal Netherlands Indies Army Air Division

This force, known by its Dutch acronym of ML-KNIL, consisted of nearly 230 combat aircraft (95 bombers, 99 fighters, and 34 reconnaissance planes) organized into five groups. Each group consisted of between one and four squadrons. Three of the groups were equipped with bombers and two with fighters. There was also a Depot Group responsible for training, transport, and support.

I Group was equipped with Glenn Martin 139 bombers. Its two squadrons were initially based on Borneo and Java. II Group was also equipped with Martin 139 bombers and its single squadron was based on Java. III Group also had the Martin 139 bomber with two squadrons on Java and one on Singapore. A fourth squadron was formed in December 1941. The two fighter groups were equipped with a mix of Brewster 339 Buffalos, Curtiss Hawk 75A-7s, and Curtiss-Wright CW-21Bs. IV Group had two squadrons based on Java and

This photo shows a 36 Squadron aircraft dropping a torpedo in the Johore Strait during prewar training. With a top speed of only 143mph, the aircraft was shockingly vulnerable to fighter interception. Accordingly, the RAF was careful about committing these aircraft but on December 26 it threw them against a Japanese convoy off Endau. The result was a massacre of the two Vildebeest squadrons. (Andrew Thomas Collection)

a third on the island of Ambon. The V Group was equipped entirely with Buffalos. Two squadrons were stationed on Borneo and a third on Singapore.

The rapid expansion of the ML-KNIL from 1936 until the start of the war and the fact that the Netherlands was occupied by the Germans after May 1940 imposed severe difficulties on the Dutch. The number of pilots could never keep up with demands. Pilots were acquired from among Dutch military personnel or from external sources. In order to increase the numbers, short- and long-term contracts were offered for officer and NCO pilots. After the Netherlands was occupied, more opportunities were opened for indigenous personnel. Training time was also reduced. Efforts to raise more fighter squadrons were increased. Bomber pilots were re-roled as fighter pilots and new pilots were sent to fighter units. Training was incomplete since the lack of experienced instructors meant that no tactical combat training was provided. Bomber squadrons were also short of aircrew, which meant that the usual five-man crew for the Martin 139 was reduced to four. Bomber squadrons

The mainstay bomber of the ML-KNIL was the Glenn Martin Model 139. This is a prewar photograph of a significant portion of the Martin force at Andir Airfield on Java. By 1941, the Martin was slow and poorly armed but could carry a respectable bomb load. Overall, it was obsolete and performed poorly during the campaign. (Netherlands Institute for Military History)

typically were composed of 11 bombers and 80 aircrew. In all squadrons, turnover was high with experienced aircrew and maintenance personnel being transferred to new squadrons and replaced by new personnel with minimal training.

Buffalos were the primary fighter aircraft of the ML-KNIL. Seventy-two B-339Ds were delivered between March and June 1941. Twenty B-439 variants with a more powerful engine were ordered but not all arrived before the fall of the NEI. The Dutch ordered 24 Curtiss-Wright CW-21 fighters in early 1940 but the fall of the Netherlands disrupted their delivery. The aircraft were diverted to the NEI where they began to arrive in October 1940. The aircraft possessed a respectable rate of climb and good maneuverability but were slow and unarmored. The aircraft was well-armed with two 12.7mm and two 7.7mm machine guns. The Curtiss-Hawk 75A-7 arrived in the NEI in the summer of 1940. This was the first monoplane fighter ordered for the ML-KNIL but enough arrived to equip only a

Only 24 Curtiss-Wright CW-21 fighters were available in the NEI. The aircraft was designed as an interceptor, but it proved unable to take damage and was not well liked by the Dutch. (Netherlands Institute for Military History)

In 1940, the Dutch began to receive 20 Curtiss Hawk 75A-7 fighters, the export version of the USAAF's P-36. The fighter remained viable at the start of the war but was hampered by serviceability issues. (Netherlands Institute for Military History)

The standard ordnance for Dutch bombers was the 300lb bomb shown here. The Glenn Martin could not carry torpedoes, which reduced its effectiveness for maritime strike. Dutch bombing accuracy was very poor during the campaign, accounting for only two transports and a minesweeper. (Netherlands Institute for Military History)

single squadron. This was the export version of the P-36 in USAAF service and was the first monoplane design of the Curtiss Hawk line of fighters. First exported in 1938, it remained valuable in 1941. It was under-armed since it carried only four 7.7mm machine guns. The Wright Cyclone engine was plagued by maintenance issues which kept serviceability rates low. Late in the campaign, the Dutch acquired some 20–24 Hurricane Mk IIbs from the RAF.

The standard Dutch bomber was the Glenn Martin 139. These were ordered in 1936 and by March 1940, 121 had been delivered and 95 were assigned to squadrons. The aircraft was called the B-10 in USAAF service. When it first entered service in 1934, it was a world-class aircraft with its all-metal monoplane design, high speed, rotating gun turrets, and internal bomb bay. By 1941, the design was obsolete. It had a top speed of only 213mph and was lightly armed with only three .30in machine guns. The Dutch were the main export operators of the export version which came in several variants. The Model 139WH-1 was delivered in February 1937 and the WH-2 variant in March 1938. The final version was the Model 139WH-3 and 3A which had improved engines and other modifications. The Dutch ordered 162 North American B-25C-5-NAs to replace them but they never reached the NEI.

The Marine Luchtvaart Dienst (MLD)

The Dutch Navy also had a dedicated naval air force composed of flying boats. Missions included antisubmarine patrol, convoy and fleet escort, reconnaissance, and minelaying. Most of the force was obsolescent but the large, rugged Dornier Do 24 was still a useful

Typical of the MLD's dated aircraft inventory was the Fokker T.IV, which entered service in 1927. Though designed as a torpedo bomber, its top speed of 160mph restricted its use to local patrols and air-sea rescue missions during the campaign. (Netherlands Institute for Military History)

aircraft. The flying boats were spread around the NEI in flights of three aircraft to cover strategic ports and straits. The backbone of the force was the eight flights equipped with the Do 24. However, this aircraft was becoming hard to support since the supply of parts had been cut off with the German occupation of the Netherlands in May 1940. In 1940, the Dutch ordered 48 Consolidated Model 28-5MNE Catalina flying boats to replace the Do 24s. These were the export version of the USN's famous PBY-5 Catalina. A total of 35 Catalinas reached the NEI before the fall of Java but the number of aircraft that entered service was limited by shortages in trained aircrew, which meant that the Do 24 remained the MLD's mainstay aircraft. Overall, the MLD was a well-trained force which was forced to fly obsolescent aircraft.

MLD Aircraft Available December 7, 1941	
Type	Operational
Fokker T.IV	10
Fokker C.XI-W	8
Fokker C.XIV-W	10
Do 15	6
Do 24K	34
Model 28-5MNE Catalina	Approx. 22
Note: the MLD also had 80 Douglas DB-7B/C light bombers on order which the Dutch intended to use as torpedo bombers. Six arrived in Java just before the Dutch surrender.	

Militaire Luchtvaart van het Koninklijk Nederlands Indisch Leger (MLKNIL) Order of Battle	
Unit	Location
I Group	
1 Squadron (Martin 139WH-3/3A)	Java
2 Squadron (Martin 139WH-3/3A)	Samarinda
II Group	
1 Squadron (Martin 139WH-2/3/3A)	Singosari
III Group	
1 Squadron (Martin 139WH-3/3A)	Singapore
2 Squadron (Martin 139WH-2)	Kalidjati
3 Squadron (Martin 139WH-3/3A)	Singapore
7 Squadron (Martin 139WH-2/3/3A)	Established December 1941
IV Group	
1 Squadron (Curtiss Hawk 75A-7)	Tjililitan
2 Squadron (Curtiss-Wright CW-21B)	Surabaya
3 Squadron (Brewster 339D)	Ambon
V Group	
1 Squadron (Brewster 339D)	Samarinda
2 Squadron (Brewster 339)	Singkawang
3 Squadron (Brewster 339D)	Singapore
VI Group	
Various trainers and transports	Java
Total Aircraft Strength Assigned to Operational Units on December 1, 1941	
Martin 139 (all variants) bomber	95
Brewster Buffalo fighter	63
Hawk 75A-7 fighter	16
CW-21B fighter	20
CW-22 reconnaissance aircraft	34

United States Army Air Force

It is almost forgotten that the USAAF fought in the NEI. Headquarters for the USAAF Far East Air Force did not arrive on Java until January 14. The relatively few aircraft sent to defend Java were forced to operate on a logistical shoestring. The lack of communications and the distances involved meant that the tactical commander exercised a high degree of independence from his chain of command.

The long-range B-17 heavy bomber was the first American aircraft to operate in the NEI. Initial operations were carried out by the 19th Bombardment Group equipped with B-17Ds and Es. By January 1, 1942, ten of the 14 B-17s which were withdrawn from the Philippines to Australia were deployed to Singosari Airfield in eastern Java for operations. The facility had a long but unpaved runway and lacked any radar or antiaircraft protection. The second bomber unit to arrive was the 7th Bombardment Group. It began operations from Malang Airfield in eastern Java on January 16 with a strength of six B-17s and four LB-30s (the export version of the B-24). These aircraft suffered from a lack of spare parts and maintenance personnel. The aircraft were older and needed overhaul. By February 1, 15 more B-17Es and four LB-30s reached Java. About the same time, the ground crews of the 7th Bombardment Group finally arrived, which went a long way to resolving some of the most severe maintenance issues. Five more B-17Es and two LB-30s reached Java in the first week of February. Both the B-17 and the LB-30 were heavy four-engine bombers with a heavy payload and long range.

The USAAF had plans to deploy a large fighter force consisting of nine squadrons of P-40Es to the NEI. These plans never came to fruition because of the speed of the Japanese advance and the massive difficulties of moving such a large force from the United States. Units were shipped out as quickly as possible but this haste invariably meant that personnel and their equipment failed to arrive at the same place at the same time and when they did unite, critical tools and parts were invariably missing.

The first P-40 unit to be sent to the NEI was the 17th Pursuit Squadron (Provisional). The flying echelon of this unit departed Brisbane on January 16 and arrived on Java on January 25. Of the 17 P-40Es dispatched, only 13 arrived. The second unit, the 20th

A USAAF P-40E photographed in Australia being assembled. The air route to Java was difficult and subject to attack by the Japanese. As a result, only some 36 aircraft reached Java. The P-40E was considered superior to the British Hurricane so was the best Allied fighter of the campaign. If flown using the proper tactics, it could rival the Japanese Zero. (Peter Ingram Collection)

USAAF Order of Battle	
7th Bombardment Group (Heavy)	(Assigned aircraft – 39 B-17Es and 12 LB-30s (export version of the B-24); there were also a handful of older B-17D and B-17C aircraft)
19th Bombardment Group (Heavy)	
91st Bombardment Squadron (Light)	(Assigned aircraft – A-24s)
3rd Pursuit Squadron (Provisional) (incorporated into the 17th Pursuit Squadron)	(Assigned aircraft – P-40Es)
17th Pursuit Squadron (Provisional)	
20th Pursuit Squadron (Provisional)	

Pursuit Squadron (Provisional) departed Darwin on February 4 with 13 P-40Es. Twelve of these reached Bali, where they were caught by a Japanese air attack which destroyed five of them. Eight more fighters from the 20th departed for Java days later and six reached their destination. The 3rd Pursuit Squadron (Provisional) followed next. The first echelon of nine P-40Es met disaster when it reached Timor on February 9. The airfield was closed because of the weather conditions, but the aircraft lacked the fuel to return to Darwin so all nine crashed onto the airfield in forced landings. Nine more fighters from the 3rd succeeded in reaching Java on February 11. The P-40Es which reached Java were incorporated into the 17th Pursuit Squadron. The new squadron was over its authorized strength of 18 fighters but the lack of early warning of impending air attacks and inadequate communications equipment severely hampered its ability to provide air defense for Surabaya.

The Curtiss P-40 was the best Allied fighter in the Far East. The version sent to Java was the P-40E which had a heavy armament of six wing-mounted .50-caliber machine guns. These could tear any Japanese aircraft to pieces. It was faster than most Japanese fighters and was much better protected, meaning it could take considerable punishment and still get its pilot home.

The P-40 could hold its own against the most modern Japanese fighters, including the formidable Zero. If proper tactics were used to capitalize on the P-40's superior speed, especially in a dive, and to avoid the strengths of the more maneuverable and faster-climbing Japanese fighters, the P-40 could be victorious, as shown by the operations on the American Volunteer Group flying out of southern China and Burma with P-40Bs. However, the unit sent to Java was trained in more traditional tactics which called for turning dogfights. Against the lighter and more maneuverable Japanese fighters, this was the worst possible tactic.

The Far East Air Force also operated the A-24 Banshee which was the Army version of the famous USN SBD Dauntless dive-bomber. Fifty-two of these aircraft were on the way to the Philippines when the war began. They were diverted to Australia and assembled. They were assigned to the 91st Bombardment Squadron (L) which was sent to Java from February 9, 1942. By February 19, seven A-24s were operational at the new airfield of Modjokerto west of Malang. Serviceability of the aircraft was hampered by missing parts and a lack of spare parts. After a brief period on Java, the squadron was ordered to depart for Australia in early March.

A small number of A-24 Banshees of the 91st Bombardment Squadron reached Java in February and were employed against the Japanese invasion force off Bali on February 19. The squadron did not receive sufficient logistical support and was withdrawn in March. (Peter Ingram Collection)

CAMPAIGN OBJECTIVES

Japanese attack plans

The most numerous IJAAF fighter during the campaign was the Nakajima Ki-27. It was a small, nimble aircraft as can be seen from this photograph of a Ki-27 assigned to the 64th Sentai in 1939. Its restricted range proved troublesome for the Japanese during the campaign. Nevertheless, it still played an important role when bases were available to bring it into action. (Andrew Thomas Collection)

The Malaya campaign

The Japanese had no existing plans to invade Malaya as tensions with the Western powers increased throughout 1941. Concrete planning began only in July 1941. This was accomplished in three phases. The broad outline was drafted by the Imperial Army's General Staff Headquarters. Once a draft was complete, discussions began with the Imperial Navy which had to synchronize its planning with that of the army. These discussions, occurring in September and October, resulted in a Basic Agreement. On November 10, the two services formally agreed on the plan to invade Malaya.

Concurrently, the IJA's 25th Army, assigned responsibility for the actual invasion, was working on a draft operational plan which was completed on November 3. The commander of the 25th Army was Lieutenant General Yamashita Tomoyuki, who was newly appointed in this critical role on November 6. His reputation was that of an excellent operational commander, which made him ideally suited for the job. Another reason was probably his ability and willingness to work with the IJAAF and the rival IJN. After assuming his new job, Yamashita spent six days in Tokyo going over the plan with General Staff Headquarters. Following this, he flew to Saigon to review the plan with the 25th Army staff, officers from the 3rd Air Division, and Vice Admiral Ozawa Jisaburo who commanded the naval forces of the Southern Expeditionary Force.

The 25th Army's plan was modified by intelligence gained in late October. On October 20, Colonel Tsuji Masanobu, Chief of Operations and Planning Staff of the 25th Army, conducted a secret reconnaissance flight over southern Thailand and northern Malaya. The flight was conducted in a new Mitsubishi Ki-46 reconnaissance aircraft which was immune to interception. The first flight was unsuccessful since heavy clouds covered Kota Bharu and when fuel ran low the mission was aborted. The next mission two days later gave the Japanese a wealth of intelligence. The Ki-46 overflew the intended landing areas of Singora and Patani in southern Thailand and then the RAF airfields at Kota Bharu, Alor Star, Sungei Patani, and Taiping. Tsuji was surprised to find the airfields to be more developed than expected. He judged it necessary to capture Kota Bharu and Alor Star as soon as possible to give the 3rd Air Division room to operate. He recommended that the operational plan be modified so that the 5th Division should land simultaneously at Singora and Patani and that it then move quickly to seize the bridge across the Perak River to capture the airfield at Alor Star. Simultaneously, elements of the 18th Division would land at Kota Bharu to seize that airfield. Tsuji believed that if British air power was staged out of Kota Bharu it could make the landings in southern Thailand impossible. The forces which seized Kota Bharu should attack south along the east coast to capture the airfield at Kuantan. The final operations order for the invasion, issued on November 23, reflected Tsuji's recommendations.

As might be expected, the planning process struggled to incorporate the different views of the IJA and IJN. The enduring rivalry between the two services played a role, but more significant was the friction created by the IJN's objectives to deliver the invasion force safely and create the conditions for successful reinforcement and resupply operations and the IJA's desire to have as large a force as possible delivered as quickly as possible to facilitate follow-on operations.

One of the most pressing planning concerns was the shortage of shipping. Available shipping was barely adequate to land the 25th Army and then support it for a campaign down the peninsula toward Singapore. The IJA wanted to land at Kota Bharu at the same time as the main landing force was coming ashore in southern Thailand. As pointed out by Tsuji, Kota Bharu needed to be occupied to protect the landing force from air attack and to permit the staging of 3rd Air Division units to the air base as soon as possible. Landing at both places at the same time was risky since it divided naval and air cover. Yamashita and Ozawa agreed on November 18 that the benefits of seizing Kota Bharu early outweighed the risks. The IJN agreed to provide more air cover and to spread the landing operation at Kota Bharu over two nights with the transports retiring to sea during the day. The shortage of shipping made Yamashita release one of the 25th Army's divisions for employment elsewhere (eventually Burma). This was a particularly bold move since it left just two whole and the majority of a third division for the entire campaign. This meant that the defenders would outnumber the attackers. But this decision also allowed Yamashita to conduct the campaign the way he wanted. The first draft of the plan was very conservative and was rejected by Yamashita because it delayed an assault on Singapore for five weeks to consolidate beachheads in southern Thailand and northern Malaya, move in additional supplies, and forward deploy the 3rd Air Division. Only after this was done would the advance on Singapore begin. This methodical approach was not in keeping with Yamashita's command style. The final plan reflected Yamashita's preference for what he called a "driving charge" – that is to seize the initiative and never give the defenders a pause. This would prevent the British forces from digging in and establishing a firm defense and give them insufficient time for reinforcements.

Yamashita's "driving charge" was a brilliant choice since it emphasized the strengths of the 25th Army and attacked the critical weakness of British forces – their need for reinforcements. It was still risky since it featured a smaller force attacking a larger one on a logistical shoestring. One of the primary reasons why this was even considered was the assumption that the Japanese would gain control of the air quickly. The IJAAF, operating initially from bases in southern Indochina, was ordered to achieve air control by crippling British air forces in northern Malaya. Immediately following the landing in southern Thailand and at Kota Bharu, IJAAF units would move to these newly captured bases to intensify the pressure on the RAF. Once air superiority was gained, the IJAAF would provide direct support to the 25th Army as it headed south.

Another reason why seizing forward air bases was so important was the short operational radius of the Ki-27, which still represented the bulk of the IJAAF's fighter

Seaplane carriers *Chitose* and *Mizuho* were assigned to the 11th Seaplane Tender Division and played an important role during the campaign. This is *Chitose* pictured before the war. It was a large, fast, and well-armed ship, designed to operate float planes in direct support of fleet and invasion operations. Its importance is shown by the number of operations it participated in during the campaign. These included the occupations of Bangka Roads, Kema, Menado, Kendari, and Ambon. *Chitose* was also present during the final invasion of Java. Its F1M2 biplane aircraft shot down a Dutch flying boat and damaged the USN destroyer *Pope*, leading to its destruction. *Chitose* was later converted to an aircraft carrier and was sunk in 1944 at the battle of Leyte Gulf. (Naval History and Heritage Command)

force. This was so important that ground crews of the 3rd Air Division were included in the initial waves at Singora and Kota Bharu. Once established in Thailand and Malaya, the 3rd Air Division had to constantly stage aircraft southward to cover the rapid advance of the 25th Army.

The IJNAF's main mission was not to provide direct support to the 25th Army, but it still had an important role to play. Naval air units would cover the invasion convoys from RAF air attack and from naval attack from the Royal Navy. The IJN had just completed an intense internal debate on force allocation for the initial phase of the Pacific War. The IJN's two main operations were conducting the critical attack into Malaya and the NEI to secure the natural resources necessary to continue the war and the surprise attack against the USN's Pacific Fleet in Pearl Harbor. At issue was the allocation of the IJN's six fleet carriers. Admiral Yamamoto, commander of the Combined Fleet, wanted all six fleet carriers to deliver a crushing blow at Pearl Harbor. The Naval General Staff wanted to retain some for the Southern Operation against Malaya and the NEI. In the end, Yamamoto bullied the Naval General Staff by threatening to resign unless all six carriers were assigned to his operation against Pearl Harbor. The Naval General Staff acquiesced to this partly because of the realization that long-range land-based aircraft would be adequate to support the offensive.

Three IJNAF air flotillas were assigned to support the Southern Operation. Of these, two were initially allocated to support the invasion of the Philippines and then the seizure of the NEI; the third was allocated to support the Malayan campaign. In addition to having the responsibility for protecting the invasion convoys from air attack, their primary mission was to assist in IJN operations to gain sea control. This mission became paramount when the Royal Navy deployed Force Z, which included two capital ships, to the region in November. IJN land-based air forces also had responsibility for assisting the IJAAF in pressuring Singapore by attacking the air and naval bases there.

The Netherlands East Indies campaign

While the Malaya campaign was mainly an IJA operation, the seizure of the NEI was run primarily by the IJN. Significant ground forces were involved, particularly in the final attack on Java, but the pace of the campaign and its ultimate success was decided by the ability of the Japanese to move occupation forces through the region by sea and cover them with air and naval forces. The overriding imperative was that the campaign be conducted as quickly as possible. The Dutch could not be given adequate time to destroy the key economic facilities in the region, and the Americans and British could not be allowed the time to reinforce the NEI, which might prolong the campaign.

Seizing Java was the ultimate objective of the NEI campaign. However, before that attack could occur, several preconditions had to be met. First, the flank and rear of the Japanese thrust had to be protected. This condition was fulfilled in the west by the rapid pace of the offensive in Malaya, where British forces were quickly crushed in northern Malaya and air superiority was gained over the RAF; in the east American air power was quickly eliminated in the Philippines.

Royal Netherlands East Indies Naval Air Force			
Unit	Aircraft	Strength	Location
GVT-1	Do 24K	3	Pontianak
GVT-2	Do 24K	3	Sorang
GVT-2 (new, formed January 19)	Catalina	3	Emmerhaven
GVT-3	Do 24K	3	Surabaya
GVT-3 (new, formed January 19)	Catalina	3	Morokrembangan
GVT-4	Do 24K	3	Sambas
GVT-5	Do 24K	3	Ternate
GVT-5 (new, formed January 12)	Catalina	3	Morokrembangan
GVT-6	Do 24K	3	Morokrembangan
GVT-7	Do 24K	3	Tarakan
GVT-7 (new, formed February from aircraft from disbanded flights)	Do 24K	4	Morokrembangan
GVT-8	Do 24K	3	Paeloe Samboe
GVT-11	Fokker T.IV	3	Morokrembangan
GVT-12	Fokker T.IV	3	Morokrembangan
GVT-16	Catalina	3	Tandjong Priok
GVT-17	Catalina	3	Ambon
GVT-18	Catalina	3	Tandjong Priok

The final attack on Java was planned as a double envelopment in which landings would occur on both ends of the island. Each of these two drives was synchronized with the other. Both used the same principle as the IJA's advance through Malaya – maintain constant pressure on the enemy, keep him off balance with the dual thrust strategy, and then mass forces for a final decision at the ultimate objective.

While the pace of the Japanese advance was relentless, each step was calculated to bring overwhelming force to bear at each objective. The entire offensive through the NEI was based on the ability of the IJN's two air flotillas to cover the advance. These two formations, the 23rd Air Flotilla (initially based on Jolo between Mindanao and Borneo) and the 21st Air Flotilla (initially flying out of Davao on Mindanao) were the linchpins of the entire operation. The Japanese planned to gain air superiority over key Allied naval and air bases, and then seize them with amphibious forces. Once the air flotillas moved up to occupy the seized airfield, the process would be repeated again. At no time did the Japanese intend to move against an objective that was not within range of friendly air cover. There was some risk involved in this approach because it required a high level of coordination and it assumed that relatively small forces could provide continual coverage of the vast expanse of the NEI. Had the Allied forces facing them possessed a better command and control structure and adequate naval and air forces to exploit opportunities, the Japanese advance might have been halted, or more likely delayed. The Japanese, however, correctly assessed that the Allies lacked the capability to exploit any temporary Japanese weakness.

Dutch Antiaircraft Guns
A total of four 105mm and 28 80mm guns were available on fixed mounts augmented by 40 40mm mobile Bofors guns. Small numbers of Rheinmetal 20mm guns reached the NEI before May 1940. All were placed around ports and other key targets on Java. In the first week of February, the British augmented antiaircraft defenses on Java with nine 40mm guns and nine 3.7in guns.

The central thrust against the NEI opened with an advance, covered by aircraft from Jolo and Davao, against Tarakan on the eastern side of Borneo. This thrust would then continue down the Makassar Strait with landings scheduled for Balikpapan and finally

Bandjermasin on southern Borneo. The eastern thrust was also staged from Davao but was targeted against the invaluable naval and air bases on the Celebes. The first landing was planned against Menado in the northwestern Celebes. From there, landings on Kendari and Makassar would follow. The seizure of Kendari was especially important. Not only was there a large anchorage nearby, but the large airbase would provide flank protection against any attack from Australia and, most importantly, put the main Allied naval base at Surabaya in eastern Java within range of land-based bombers and fighters. Once southern Celebes were occupied, the Japanese would be in a position to cut off the NEI from reinforcement from Australia and strike Ambon Island, which the Japanese knew was the location of an Allied bomber base. The seizure of Koepang on Timor Island and Denpasar on Bali would cut the direct air reinforcement route from Australia. In the final phase of the campaign, the covering air and naval forces from the central and eastern thrusts, basically the same units used in a sequential manner, would then combine to escort the invasion force slated to land on eastern Java.

The other wing of the Japanese advance to Java was provided by the naval forces covering the advance into Malaya. In addition to supporting the Malaya invasion force, it was planned to use these forces to seize key points on western Borneo. After supporting the Japanese advance down Malaya, these forces would also conduct operations against southern Sumatra. The final task of these forces was to form the western part of the pincer attack against Java.

In addition to the IJNAF land-based air flotillas, a light carrier and a number of seaplane carriers and tenders supported the Japanese advance. These ships provided important support against the sporadic air resistance offered by the Dutch; this level of support, backed by the land-based air flotillas, was judged to be sufficient to cover the many amphibious operations.

British defense plans

British defense planning in the Far East was predicated on the need for a strong Royal Navy presence to secure British interests and, if necessary, defeat a Japanese attack. Since the Royal Navy was not large enough after World War I to station a large fleet in the Far East permanently, the planning assumption was that a fleet would be dispatched from European waters in a period of crisis. The general view was that the fleet would be in the main naval base of Singapore within 70 days after London decided that it was necessary to send one. This optimistic view was undermined by events in Europe, with the rise of Germany and tensions with the Italians in the Mediterranean. These forced a revaluation of the assumption that the fleet could quickly be sent to Singapore. By May 1939, the British admitted to the Australians that they could no longer be certain when such a fleet would be dispatched or how powerful it would be. In July 1939, the projected time for the fleet to arrive was lengthened from 70 to 90 days. After the war in Europe began in September, the Chiefs of Staff in London informed the authorities in Malaya that it could take as long as six months for the fleet to arrive. In reality, even this was impossible following the fall of France in June 1940 and the entry of the Italians into the war.

With the Royal Navy no longer able to come to the rescue of British possessions in the Far East, the primary responsibility for the defense of Malaya shifted to the Army and the RAF. Not only did the Army and the RAF have to bear the burden of defense, but they would have to do so for a prolonged period. Both agreed it was absolutely vital to hold the naval base on Singapore. By 1938, all services agreed that the defense of Singapore meant defending Malaya as well in order to keep the naval base out of enemy air and artillery range. Even after they came to this epiphany, the army and the RAF were unable to coordinate their strategies. The RAF continued to build bases in Malaya, including several in northern Malaya near the border with Thailand. This forced the army to disperse its defenses to protect bases that the RAF lacked the aircraft to use fully.

The RAF saw itself as the premier service in the Far East once it was apparent that the RN could not send a large fleet to the region. The RAF contended that aircraft offered the best option for dealing with an invasion force. To be successful, the RAF had to maintain air superiority while delivering crushing strikes as far from Malaya as possible over a period of several days. This drove the decision to place the flying squadrons as far forward as possible. The RAF promised the army that it would inflict 40 percent attrition on the invasion force before it reached the coast.

The number of aircraft required to defend Malaya kept growing in British defense planning. In 1940, RAF forces in Malaya totaled a pathetic 88 aircraft in eight squadrons. The first estimate from the Chiefs of Staff in London declared a need for 336 aircraft. This was questionable from the start since it was assessed at the time that the Japanese could commit some 700 aircraft against Malaya. RAF authorities in Malaya thought they needed 556 aircraft. In spite of these plans, only 188 were available at the start of the war. Even more problematic was the lack of a reliable reinforcement route to move a continuous stream of new aircraft to the region.

As the size of RAF Far East Command doubled in 1941, there were still tremendous shortcomings. The staff was too small and inexperienced to be effective. There were not enough operational aircraft and too few in reserve. The air defense command was not fully functional, and the numbers of fighters and antiaircraft guns were inadequate. The fighters which were available were obsolescent. Only a handful of reconnaissance aircraft was available. While maritime strike was viewed as a critical mission, only some 30 obsolete torpedo aircraft were on hand when hostilities commenced. Brooke-Popham foresaw a possible campaign unfolding in which the RAF could not stop a Japanese invasion and then lacked the staying power for a prolonged battle.

British prewar defense planning for the defense of Malaya was incoherent. Most of all, the British planners in London and Singapore failed to understand the kind of campaign the Japanese were planning to fight. Yamashita's "driving strategy" accepted the risk of running a major offensive on a logistical shoestring, something the British could not foresee the Japanese doing. The British assessed that even if the Japanese did attack and get a major force ashore in Malaya, it would not be able to advance fast enough to threaten Singapore before the British could bring in significant reinforcements. The British notion that Singapore could be held against an enemy with control of the air and sea was sheer fantasy. The stage was set for Britain's greatest military disaster.

Dutch defense plans

Dutch authorities in the NEI had few options when it came to planning against a possible Japanese invasion. Available Dutch forces were totally inadequate to defend the expanse of the NEI. Dutch naval power was weak, and with their homeland under German occupation the Dutch were barely able to maintain what they had, much less grow their naval capabilities. The same held true for Dutch air forces in the NEI. The Dutch were forced to procure aircraft wherever they could, which usually meant obtaining second-rate American aircraft. The size of the Dutch ground force was clearly inadequate to cover the entire NEI and much of the force was made up of native personnel whose will to fight was unknown. The only Dutch hope was the promise of British or American help to defend them. Military talks began with the British in November 1940 and with the Americans in April 1941, but the Dutch were unable to secure any firm commitments. The British could hardly defend their own possessions in the Far East and the neutral Americans could not make promises to come to the aid of the Dutch. By late 1941, the Dutch were totally dependent on the British politically, which translated to military dependence as well. The British leaned on the Dutch to promise to assist in the defense of Singapore, which the Dutch agreed was an absolute priority that came before anything else.

Given the weakness of Dutch ground forces in the NEI, the key to a successful defense was the application of air and naval power against the invading Japanese. If Allied naval and air forces were unable to inflict significant attrition on a Japanese naval invasion force and a Japanese landing force got ashore, the prospect for a successful defense by the Dutch East Indies Army was low. This became the pattern throughout the NEI campaign. Once the Japanese seized the objective it provided them with a base for subsequent operations.

Japanese Orders of Battle (December 8, 1941)

Imperial Japanese Navy Air Force		
21st Air Flotilla (based on Formosa)		
Kanoya Air Group	G4M	27
1st Air Group	G3M	36
Toko Air Group (detachment)	H6K	24
22nd Air Flotilla (based near Saigon, Indochina)		
Genzan Air Group	G3M	36
Mihoro Air Group	G3M	36
Kanoya Air Group (detachment)	G4M	27
Yamada Unit		
A6M2	25	
A5M4	12	
C5M	6	
23rd Air Flotilla (based on Formosa)		
Takao Air Group	G4M	54
Tainan Air Group	A6M2	45
	A5M	12
	C5N	6
3rd Air Group	A6M2	45
	A5M4	12
	C5N	6
Carrier		
Ryujo (Air group: 12 (+ 4 spares) A5M4 fighters and 14 B5N (+ 4 spares) (12 N1 and 2 N2) attack planes)		
Seaplane carriers		
Chitose (Air group: up to 24 F1M2s and E13A1s)		
Mizuho (Air group: up to 24 F1M2s and E13A1s)		
Seaplane tenders		
Kamikawa Maru (Air group: 14 F1M2s and E13A1s)		
Sagara Maru (Air group: 6 F1M2 and 2 Kawanishi Type 95 E8N2 two-seat float biplanes)		
Sanuki Maru (Air group: 6 E8N2s (2 more in reserve))		
Sanyo Maru (Air group: 6 F1M2s and 2 E13A1s with 2 Kawanishi Type 95 E8N2s in reserve)		

Imperial Japanese Army Air Force		
3rd Air Division		
3rd Air Brigade		
59th Sentai	Ki-43	24
27th Sentai	Ki-51	23
75th Sentai	Ki-48	25
90th Sentai	Ki-48/Ki-30	30
7th Air Brigade		
64th Sentai	Ki-43/Ki-27	35/6
12th Sentai	Ki-21	21
60th Sentai	Ki-21	39
98th Sentai	Ki-21	42
10th Air Brigade		
77th Sentai	Ki-27	27
31st Sentai	Ki-30	24
62nd Sentai	Ki-21	22
70th Independent Chutai	Ki-15	8
12th Air Brigade		
1st Sentai	Ki-27	42
11th Sentai	Ki-27	39
81st Sentai	Ki-15/Ki-46	9/7
15th Independent Hikotai		
50th Independent Chutai	Ki-15/Ki-46	5
51st Independent Chutai	Ki-15/Ki-46	6
83rd Independent Hikotai (all en route)		
71st Independent Chutai	Ki-51	10
73rd Independent Chutai	Ki-51	9
89th Independent Chutai	Ki-36	12
Units under direct command of the Southern Army		
21st Independent Hikotai		
84th Independent Chutai	Ki-27	9
82nd Independent Chutai	Ki-48	12
Others		
47th Independent Chutai	Ki-44	9
1st, 2nd, 13th, 15th Transport Units		

THE CAMPAIGN

Imperial Japan's advance south

The battle for northern Malaya

It took the Japanese only two days to secure air superiority over northern Malaya. The RAF made an all-out effort to repel the Japanese invasion of southern Thailand and northern Malaya but failed totally.

The first actual casualties of the air war came before the formal opening of hostilities when 1st Sentai Ki-27s attacked an RAF Catalina flying boat on December 7 over the South China Sea to prevent it from spotting the Japanese invasion force. The Catalina's entire crew of eight was lost. In the afternoon three RAAF Hudsons did spot the approaching Japanese convoys, which gave the British warning of the imminent invasion.

When the war began on December 8, Kota Bharu was the scene of the most intense action. Three Japanese transports carrying some 5,600 men including the 56th Regiment and IJAAF ground crews began landing at 0200 hours. Seven Hudsons scrambled from Kota Bharu to conduct immediate attacks and were joined soon after by another three. In repeated attacks, all three transports were hit and damaged. Two Hudsons were shot down by antiaircraft fire. Seven Vildebeests followed for a torpedo attack but only four were able to release their torpedoes and these all missed. One Vildebeest crashed on landing and was damaged beyond repair. Most of the Japanese assault troops got ashore before the transports were forced to withdraw and after a tough fight with Indian troops were able to capture the airfield.

At Singora and Patani in southern Thailand, the landings were briefly opposed by Thai troops when the Japanese came ashore at 0400 hours. Singora Airfield was seized and at first light Ki-27s from the 1st, 11th, and 77th Sentai began to fly in. The IJA's 5th Division got ashore in good order and began its drive into northern Malaya.

The RAF planned a maximum effort against the invasion fleet during the daylight hours of December 8. Orders were given to 8 RAAF and 60 Squadrons at Kuantan, 27 Squadron at Sungei Patani, 62 Squadron at Alor Star, and 34 Squadron at Tengah to attack immediately. Number 100 Squadron was ordered to move to Kuantan and await further orders. As the

The Hudson bomber was a conversion from the Lockheed 14 Super Electra airliner. This is a Hudson I of 1 Squadron RAAF, based at Kota Bharu at the start of the war, which made continuous attacks on a three-transport Japanese invasion force offshore during the first hours of the war. As a light bomber the Hudson was mediocre because of its low top speed and light armament of two fixed machine guns in the nose and two in the dorsal turret. On the positive side, it was highly maneuverable for an aircraft of its size. (Andrew Thomas Collection)

The Blenheim IV was an improved Blenheim with a slightly higher speed, protective armor, and up to five machine guns. Its bomb load was still restricted to 1,000lb or less under operational conditions. Number 34 Squadron was equipped with the Blenheim IV at the start of the campaign, and two reinforcing squadrons also operated this bomber. This is a 211 Squadron Blenheim IV in early 1942. (Andrew Thomas Collection)

RAF executed its plan to hit the invasion fleet, the IJAAF began its counterair campaign against RAF airfields in northern Malaya.

The RAF strikes against Japanese shipping were impeded by heavy fog. For this reason, the area off Kota Bharu was the focus of attacks while the main invasion force farther north off Singora remained almost untouched. Twelve 8 RAAF Squadron Blenheims departed Kuantan at 0630 hours. When they arrived off Kota Bharu, they found *Awagisan Maru* and claimed several hits on the transport. Two bombers crash-landed on their return, one at Kota Bharu and the second at Seletar. The next RAF aircraft to make an appearance were eight Blenheim Is from 60 Squadron. These also chose the unfortunate *Awagisan Maru* for attack; it was damaged again and later sank. Zeros from the 22nd Air Flotilla tried to protect the transport, but lost one of their number to the Hudson gunners. Two Blenheims were lost to antiaircraft fire; of the six remaining, three returned to Kuantan with heavy damage.

Nine Blenheim IVs from 34 Squadron found no ships off Kota Bharu to attack so struck the landing beaches and barges instead. Defending Japanese fighters claimed one shot down which actually crash-landed at Machang. The remaining aircraft were ordered to recover at Butterworth which was under attack by IJA fighters. Two more Blenheims were lost on landing. Later in the day, four Hudsons and three Vildebeests were sent to attack a reported landing south of Kota Bharu. The report was false, so the strike ended up attacking Japanese barges off Kota Bharu.

Finding nothing at Kota Bharu to attack when they arrived at 0900 hours, the 11 Blenheim IVs from 62 Squadron headed north to Patani. They found a large number of transports defended by fighters including two F1M float planes from seaplane tender *Sagara Maru*. The Blenheims dropped their bombs through clouds with no success, but all aircraft survived. The squadron returned to Alor Star to re-arm and re-fuel but were caught on the ground by 27 Ki-21s from 60th Sentai. The bombing destroyed four Blenheims and damaged five, and fuel and buildings on the base were set aflame. Two 21 RAAF Squadron Buffalos on a reconnaissance mission were also active off Singora. They were engaged by 12 Ki-27s but both Buffalos were able to escape.

Eight Blenheim IFs with bombs from 27 Squadron attempted an early morning strike but bad weather forced them back. While they were gone the Japanese struck their base. Sungei Patani was not ready for an attack. There were no dispersal areas and no effective warning system, while only four 40mm Bofors guns defended the base. Four Buffalos from 21 RAAF Squadron were on alert but didn't take off until the first bombs fell from 27 12th Sentai Ki-21s. The Japanese bombers were accurate; three Blenheims were damaged, two Buffalos were destroyed, and five more were damaged. The main runway was knocked out of service.

Number 27 Squadron was reduced to four operational Blenheims and the last four Buffalos were ordered to Butterworth.

Butterworth also came under attack. It was strafed by Ki-43s from the 1st Chutai of the 64th Sentai. The fighters faced no antiaircraft fire and succeeded in damaging four Blenheims of 34 Squadron.

The Japanese were particularly worried about Kota Bharu being used as a staging base against the invasion convoy so it was attacked throughout the day at about 15-minute intervals by small groups of Ki-27s and Ki-43s. Ki-48s from the 15th Sentai also added to the carnage, damaging two more Hudsons. Before the airfield was captured by Japanese ground troops, the five remaining Hudsons and six Vildebeests were ordered to Kuantan. When the airfield was occupied by the Japanese, they found the runway was not destroyed and that bombs, torpedoes, and fuel were left intact. Seven Hudsons with varying degrees of damage were also left for the Japanese.

By the end of the first day, the RAF had lost the use of the key airfield at Kota Bharu. In addition, the RAF's bomber force had taken grievous losses. Japanese losses were also heavy, but most were due to operational causes. Eight aircraft were lost owing to weather-related causes, and another 18 were lost on the ground, mostly as a result of landing accidents.

The second day

On the second day of their counterair campaign, the Japanese continued to hit hard at RAF airfields. A large strike of Ki-48s escorted by Ki-43s hit the airfield at Machang. The 8th Indian Brigade, responsible for defending the area, withdrew to the south, surrendering Gong Kedah and Machang Airfields. With the capture of Kota Bharu late on the 8th, the 3rd Air Division now had three airfields in Malaya and several in southern Thailand. Alor Star Airfield was also abandoned by the RAF and the last seven serviceable Blenheims were ordered to Butterworth.

In spite of this battering, the RAF planned a strike on Singora Airfield with six Blenheims from 34 and 60 Squadrons. The strike arrived over the target in the early afternoon and was intercepted by Ki-27s of the 1st Sentai. Three Blenheims were lost; the bombers were not able to observe the results of their attack. The three surviving aircraft recovered at Butterworth. They were ordered to join with three more 62 Squadron Blenheims and conduct another attack on Singora. Before the other bombers could arrive, the station was attacked by Ki-21s and Ki-51s escorted by Ki-27s. The four Buffalos present attempted to defend the airfield but were ineffective. One was shot down immediately and another was forced to land and was strafed and destroyed on the ground. When the second pair engaged the Japanese, another Buffalo was shot down and the second was damaged and forced to land. The ensuing bombing inflicted heavy damage on the facility and destroyed several Blenheims. After the raid, the station commander ordered all remaining aircraft to depart. Two 21 RAAF Squadron Buffalos headed to Ipoh and two 62 Squadron Blenheims were dispatched to Taiping. All other Blenheims, a total of six aircraft from three squadrons, were ordered to proceed to Singapore. After only two days, the Blenheim force had been shattered. Only ten aircraft remained of the original 47, and of these only two were fully operational.

Even in the midst of disaster, the RAF continued efforts to take the fight to the Japanese. As Butterworth was being bombed, one of the Blenheims which was ordered to attack Singora managed to take off and headed to its target. The single bomber got through to the airfield and made a single bomb pass but could not observe the results. The brave crew was attacked by Japanese fighters on the way back and was forced to crash-land at Alor Star. As vulnerable as the RAF airfields were to attack, the IJAAF showed that its airfields were also vulnerable, principally because of a total lack of radar. Had the RAF had enough bombers to sustain attacks on Japanese airfields, the IJAAF would have been under great pressure.

EVENTS

1 0208–0600 hours: Hudsons in two groups from 1 RAAF Squadron depart Kota Bharu. One Hudson is shot down by antiaircraft fire. The undamaged Hudsons fly a second strike. Another Hudson is shot down by antiaircraft fire and at least five more are damaged. All three Japanese transports are heavily damaged. *Awagisan Maru* later sinks and the other two withdraw north.

2 After 0400 hours: Ki-27s from three *sentai* arrive at Singora Airfield.

3 0415 hours: 17 G3Ms from the Mihoro Air Group attack Singapore. They encounter only ineffective antiaircraft fire. Three Blenheims at Tengah Airfield are damaged.

4 Approximately 0600 hours: 36 Squadron is ordered to attack the retreating Japanese off Kota Bharu. Only four aircraft drop their torpedoes through heavy rain and antiaircraft fire, but all miss. One Vildebeest crashes on landing and is written off.

5 0630 hours: Two Buffalos from 243 Squadron strafe barges off Kota Bharu; one is damaged by ground fire.

6 0630 hours: 12 Hudsons from 8 RAAF Squadron and eight Blenheim IVs of 60 Squadron depart Kuantan. Arriving off Kota Bharu, they attack the burning *Awagisan Maru* and various small craft. One Hudson crash-lands at Kota Bharu and another damaged Hudson recovers at Seletar. Three of the six returning to Kuantan are damaged by antiaircraft fire. One Hudson claims a Zero. The Blenheims also repeat the attack on the burning transport except for one which attacks targets to the north. Two Blenheims are lost to antiaircraft fire.

7 0645 hours: Eight Blenheims from 27 Squadron take off from Sungei Patani to strike Japanese shipping but are forced back by bad weather.

8 0700 hours: at least five Ki-21s from the 98th Sentai bomb Sungei Patani. The alert Buffalos launch in the middle of the attack and then suffer gun failure so no Japanese aircraft are damaged. One Blenheim and two Buffalos are destroyed; two Blenheims and five Buffalos are damaged by bombs. The main runway is knocked out of action.

9 0700: Nine Ki-21s bomb Machang. One Buffalo delivers an ineffective attack. Ki-48s also bomb the airfield.

10 Approximately 0730 hours: Nine 34 Squadron Blenheims from Tengah attack small craft off Kota Bharu and troops ashore. Ki-43s from the 64th Sentai claim one Blenheim which actually crash-lands on Machang.

11 0900 hours: Ki-27s and Ki-43s begin strafing Kota Bharu in relays. One photo-reconnaissance Beaufort is destroyed. Other fighters and light bombers attack Machang and Gong Kedah throughout the day.

12 0900 hours: 11 Blenheim IVs from 62 Squadron take off from Alor Star. Finding no targets off Kota Bharu, they head north to Patani and bomb through clouds. Two F1Ms from *Sagara Maru* conduct an unsuccessful interception.

13 Approximately 0900 hours: The remaining 34 Squadron Blenheims arrive at Butterworth Airfield in the middle of a raid by 59th Sentai Ki-43s. One Ki-43 is shot down by return fire and one Blenheim is forced to crash-land.

14 1045 hours: 27 Ki-21s from the 12th Sentai hit Sungei Patani and inflict heavy damage. The airfield is ordered to be abandoned later in the day.

15 Approximately 1045 hours: Butterworth Airfield is strafed by 1st Chutai, 64th Sentai. Four 34 Squadron Blenheims are damaged.

16 Approximately 1100 hours: 27 60th Sentai Ki-21s hit Alor Star. Four Blenheims of the just-returned 62 Squadron are destroyed and five damaged.

17 Approximately 1200 hours: Two RAAF 21 Squadron Buffalos conduct a reconnaissance of Singora. They are intercepted by Ki-27s of the 11th Sentai, but both aircraft return.

18 Approximately 1200 hours: Four Hudsons and three Vildebeests depart Kota Bharu to attack shipping reported off the coast. The report is false, so the aircraft end up strafing ground targets.

19 1600 hours: Japanese troops approach Kota Bharu Airfield; the five remaining Hudsons and six Vildebeests are evacuated to Kuantan.

Kuantan
3
4

The First Day Over Malaya – December 8, 1941

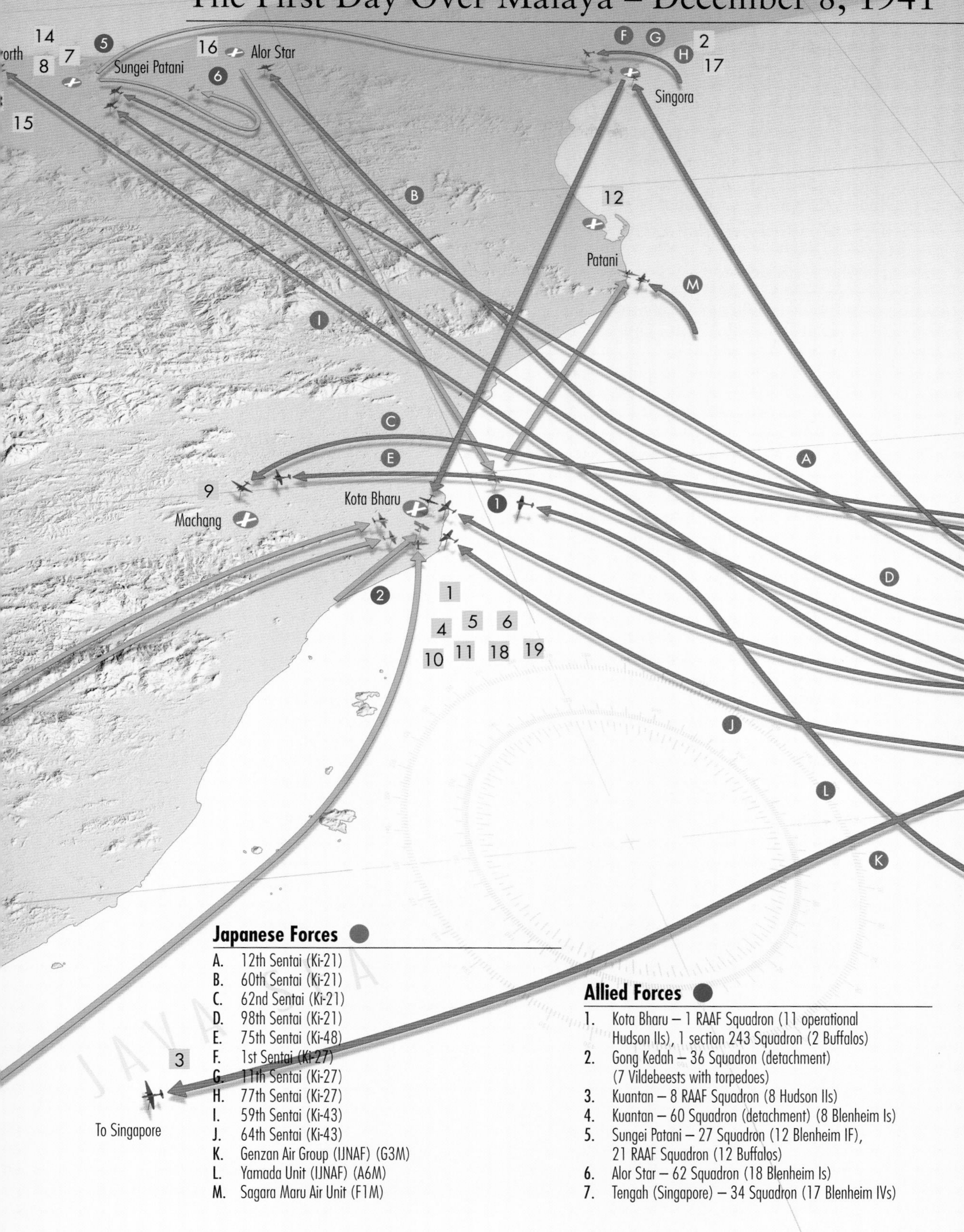

Japanese Forces

A. 12th Sentai (Ki-21)
B. 60th Sentai (Ki-21)
C. 62nd Sentai (Ki-21)
D. 98th Sentai (Ki-21)
E. 75th Sentai (Ki-48)
F. 1st Sentai (Ki-27)
G. 11th Sentai (Ki-27)
H. 77th Sentai (Ki-27)
I. 59th Sentai (Ki-43)
J. 64th Sentai (Ki-43)
K. Genzan Air Group (IJNAF) (G3M)
L. Yamada Unit (IJNAF) (A6M)
M. Sagara Maru Air Unit (F1M)

Allied Forces

1. Kota Bharu – 1 RAAF Squadron (11 operational Hudson IIs), 1 section 243 Squadron (2 Buffalos)
2. Gong Kedah – 36 Squadron (detachment) (7 Vildebeests with torpedoes)
3. Kuantan – 8 RAAF Squadron (8 Hudson IIs)
4. Kuantan – 60 Squadron (detachment) (8 Blenheim Is)
5. Sungei Patani – 27 Squadron (12 Blenheim IF), 21 RAAF Squadron (12 Buffalos)
6. Alor Star – 62 Squadron (18 Blenheim Is)
7. Tengah (Singapore) – 34 Squadron (17 Blenheim IVs)

The battle for central Malaya

After the destruction of British air power in northern Malaya, the pace of air operations slackened as the RAF re-formed in the south and the IJAAF staged aircraft forward. The RAF decided to focus fighter operations on the defense of Singapore and on providing protection to convoys. This solidified Japanese air control over northern Malaya. The ground battle was also moving quickly in favor of the Japanese. The 11th Indian Division was shattered on December 11 at the battle for Jitra, which led to the loss of northern Malaya. On December 14, the Japanese captured Alor Star Airfield virtually intact. Two days later, Penang Island was evacuated and then occupied by the Japanese.

During this period, the IJAAF kept the pressure on RAF airfields. The 25th Army's complaints that the 3rd Air Division was fighting its own war against the RAF had merit since the majority of sorties were devoted to counterair operations. The few roads in northern and central Malaya provided the IJAAF with the potential to pummel the retreating British, but interdiction was not part of the IJAAF's doctrine. The 3rd Air Division never massed air power to sustain attacks on the retreating and virtually defenseless British ground forces aside from periodic attacks by small groups of bombers. Even this relatively low level of air activity is highlighted in British accounts of the campaign and had a discernable effect on the declining morale of British ground forces.

Penang was the target of sustained attacks by 75th and 90th Sentai Ki-48s on December 12 and 13. This drove Pulford's decision on December 12 to send 453 Squadron back to Butterworth with 16 Buffalos. The RAF wanted to continue offensive counterair operations against the main Japanese airfield at Singora but this was impossible given the small number of operational bombers and the lack of fighter protection.

The IJAAF continued to move aircraft forward. Their ability to do so quickly surprised even Pulford. On December 11, the first Ki-43s from the 11th Sentai landed at Kota Bharu. By the evening of December 15, the Japanese had moved elements of the 83rd Independent Hikotai with Ki-51s and Ki-36s to the airfield along with Ki-48 light bombers. There was plenty of fuel and ordnance available, courtesy of the RAF.

The best available IJAAF light bomber was the Kawasaki Ki-48, which equipped the 75th and 90th Sentai. Though mediocre in all respects, it played an important role in the campaign conducting strikes against Allied airfields. (Philip Jarrett Collection)

Ipoh was the next RAF airfield to come under concerted attack. On December 14, the two squadrons present (453 and 21 RAAF) had no Buffalos operational. More were sent to the airfield so that there were enough for a standing patrol of four fighters on the 15th. These engaged a large raid by Ki-48s from the 90th Sentai and shot down one. On the 17th, the Japanese returned in greater strength with 59th Sentai Ki-43s and two waves of bombers. The raid was intercepted by Buffalos, but two were shot down by Japanese fighters and another forced to crash-land. The bombers destroyed two more Buffalos on the ground and damaged another. The following day, the Japanese kept up the pressure with two more raids by 59th Sentai Ki-43s and 90th Sentai Ki-48s. Two more Buffalos were destroyed on the ground and three more damaged. By the 19th, only seven Buffalos were operational at Ipoh, and two of these were caught on the ground and destroyed by a surprise bomber attack in the morning. Later in the day, the RAF abandoned Ipoh and ordered the remaining aircraft south to Kuala Lumpur.

Luckily for the IJAAF, the Ki-43 was entering service right before the war. The Ki-43 had the range required for the Malaya campaign and played a key role in the 3rd Division's counterair operations. The Japanese allocated the new fighter to two of the *sentai* allocated to the 3rd Air Division. This is a Ki-43 of the 64th Sentai preparing to take off from Kota Bharu. On December 22, 1941, the Ki-43 demonstrated its superiority over the Buffalo in a large clash with 453 Squadron. However, the pictured aircraft was lost during this encounter, probably as a result of wing cracks, which were a problem with early Ki-43s. (Andrew Thomas Collection)

On December 20, the IJAAF staged aircraft into Sungei Patani Airfield. Once again, the Japanese found vast amounts of fuel and ordnance left behind. From this base, the Japanese began to attack Kuala Lumpur. On the 21st, the first raid was mounted with 14 light bombers from the 27th and 90th Sentai escorted by 12 Ki-43s from the 59th Sentai. Two Buffalos intercepted the Japanese and claimed a bomber in exchange for one Buffalo shot down. Little damage was done to the airfield by the bombers. The following day, the Japanese returned and the largest air battle of the campaign to date ensued. Twelve Buffalos from 453 Squadron were in the air when 18 Ki-43s from the 64th Sentai arrived late in the morning. The Japanese used an altitude advantage to conduct a diving attack. Catching the British by surprise, they claimed 11 Buffalos destroyed with another four probables. This was another case of over-claiming, but the truth was bad enough – of the 12 Buffalos airborne, only six returned to Kuala Lumpur and another landed at a different airfield. Three were shot down and two others forced to crash-land. In exchange, the 64th Sentai lost an experienced *chutai* leader to a possible wing failure. Another raid later in the day by strafing Ki-43s accounted

Buffalo vs Ki-27

Air activity on December 8 was intense as the Japanese mounted continuous and widespread attacks on RAF facilities in northern Malaya and the RAF attempted to strike the Japanese landing force off Kota Bharu and Singora. 21 RAAF Squadron was based at Sungei Patani. Two of its Buffalos were ordered to conduct a reconnaissance mission over Singora. The two aircraft were intercepted by a dozen fighters with fixed undercarriages as they approached their objective. The Australians identified them as "Navy 96s" (IJN Type 96 A5M4 fighters), but they were actually Ki-27s from the 11th Sentai. The two Buffalos gave a good account of themselves against the much more maneuverable Japanese fighters. The lead pilot, Flight Lieutenant Kinninmont, reported that one Ki-27 dived on him from above and that another quickly gained position on his tail. He took his Buffalo into a dive and three Japanese fighters followed him down. After avoiding the attacks of the pursuing Japanese with a series of turns, he escaped by flying at low level toward the Malaya border. His wingman used the same tactic, and both returned to Sungei Patani. The pilots from the 11th Sentai claimed both Buffalos shot down for no losses. Many Buffalos did not survive a dogfight with the extremely maneuverable Ki-27, but on this occasion the Australians made the correct choice to make a high-speed dive to escape.

Jim Laurier

for another Buffalo destroyed on the ground. By the end of the day, 453 Squadron had only three Buffalos operational.

The ground battle for central Malaya was decided very quickly. Lieutenant General Arthur Percival, General Officer Commanding in Malaya and architect of the unsuccessful ground campaign, ordered his ground commanders to make a stand at Kampar. Percival assessed that holding the airfields in central Malaya was crucial to allow the safe arrival of several critical reinforcement convoys. The stand at Kampar lasted only four days before the British decided to withdraw to avoid encirclement. On January 3, Kuantan Airfield was abandoned. At the battle of Slim River on January 7, two Indian brigades were destroyed by a small Japanese tank force; this led to the loss of central Malaya. The next day, the British decided to withdraw to southern Malaya. Australian ground forces were introduced into the battle, but these also failed to stop the Japanese. On January 25, the British commanders decided to abandon Malaya and fall back to Singapore Island.

The IJNAF's air campaign

The IJNAF fought a largely parallel war to the IJAAF since their operations were only loosely coordinated. Its first priority was maritime targets followed by strikes on strategic targets on Singapore Island. The 22nd Air Flotilla could not devote its entire attention to supporting the counterair campaign against the RAF in Malaya since it also was responsible for supporting Japanese landings in western Borneo. During the early morning hours of December 8, the IJNAF conducted the first raid against Singapore. In this first attempt, the 34 G3Ms from the Genzan Air Group were forced to return on account of the weather conditions. The second attempt was the work of Mihoro Air Group, which launched 31 G3Ms. Fourteen were forced back by bad weather, but the other 17 got through to bomb Keppel Harbor, the naval base, and Seletar and Tengah airfields. British radar detected the incoming raid and fighters were placed on alert. They were not given the order to launch because the antiaircraft gunner requested a free field of fire. The raiders encountered only inaccurate antiaircraft fire. Most bombs hit the city, but three Blenheims of 34 Squadron were damaged at Tengah.

The IJNAF contributed to the attacks on RAF facilities on December 9. Kuantan Airfield was subjected to a heavy attack by two *chutai* of G3M bombers from the Genzan and Mihoro Air Groups. The airfield had no antiaircraft guns so the bombers proceeded to bomb and strafe unhindered. Several aircraft were destroyed including three Hudsons, two Vildebeests, and a Blenheim. Two more Hudsons and a Blenheim were damaged. After this devastating attack, all flyable aircraft were ordered to Singapore. At 1600 hours, ten Hudsons and eight Vildebeests took off and headed south. Following their departure, the ground crews evacuated the station in a panic. Large amounts of fuel and ordnance were again left behind. The station was downgraded to the status of an advanced landing ground.

The only RAF night fighters in the Far East were the 12 Blenheim IFs of 27 Squadron. Without radar, they were practically useless in their intended role and were used primarily as regular bombers during the campaign. (Andrew Thomas Collection)

The end of Force Z

When the Royal Navy dispatched *Prince of Wales* and *Repulse* to Singapore, the IJN responded by moving a detachment of 27 G4M bombers of the elite Kanoya Air

Group to Indochina. Combined with the G3Ms of the Genzan and Mihoro Air Groups, the Japanese expected that Force Z could be neutralized by air power alone. This was critical since the two British capital ships had the potential to upset the Japanese invasion timetable. The IJN had sufficient surface forces in the South China Sea to successfully engage Force Z, but if the British threat could be eliminated by air attack the uncertainties of a surface action could be avoided.

Once Force Z had been spotted, the Japanese planned for a mass attack by all three air groups. Per doctrine, the G3Ms would open the attack with horizontal bombing with the intent of softening the targets for a follow-up torpedo attack. The Japanese did not believe the bombing attacks could sink the heavily armored capital ships, but they expected that they would severely reduce Force Z's antiaircraft capabilities. The main punch would be delivered by the torpedo bombers flying some 100ft above the water and attacking the ships at right angles with the excellent Type 91 aerial torpedo. The Kanoya Air Group was expected to be especially effective since it had just completed an extensive period of torpedo training.

This Japanese photo shows the opening phases of the destruction of Force Z. Battlecruiser *Repulse* is at the top of the image surrounded by bomb explosions and battleship *Prince of Wales* is steaming at high speed at the bottom of the photo. Even the highly trained Japanese bombers were unable to inflict real damage with horizontal bombing, but subsequent attacks by torpedo bombers proved fatal to both ships. (Naval History and Heritage Command)

The contest between Japanese air power and British battleships was not long in coming. Upon receiving reports on December 8 of Japanese landings at three points in Thailand and Malaya, the commander of Force Z, Admiral (acting) Sir Tom Phillips, determined that he would have to act quickly if there was to be any hope of defeating the Japanese invasion. With the monsoon weather providing cover, Phillips departed Singapore Naval Base at dusk on the 8th, taking to sea to attack the Japanese invasion fleet off Singora. The target was later changed to Kota Bharu with the intent to arrive there on the morning of December 10. *Prince of Wales* and *Repulse* were escorted by four destroyers. Of these ships, only *Prince of Wales* had any appreciable antiaircraft capabilities and even its capability to engage low-flying aircraft was limited. Phillips was aware that he was taking a risk, but he had no idea of the true capabilities of the land-based IJNAF bombers. The true range of Japanese bombers and their abilities to deliver torpedo attacks were unknown to the Royal Navy, which expected that the Japanese would only be capable of inferior versions of horizontal bombing attacks like those delivered by the Germans and Italians.

Phillips hoped that the heavy weather would enable him to surprise the Japanese off Kota Bharu but luck was not with him. At 1345 hours, a Japanese submarine spotted Force Z and at 1740 hours the first of three Japanese aircraft spotted the British force after the skies cleared. Phillips did not cancel the operation until just after 2000 hours. He ordered Force Z to head south to Singapore some 275 miles away. This changed at 2355 hours when a report reached *Prince of Wales* that a Japanese landing had occurred at Kuantan. The report was entirely false, but since it was only 120 miles from Force Z's current location, Phillips decided to investigate it. Kuantan was some 450 miles from the nearest IJNAF air base, which was beyond the range of effective air attack in Phillips' mind. Phillips did not request fighter cover for this change of plan since he did not want to break radio silence and thought his Chief of Staff in Singapore, in receipt of the same report, would know he was headed to Kuantan

In this poor-quality Japanese photograph, Force Z is shown maneuvering under attack with a destroyer in the foreground and *Prince of Wales* and *Repulse* in the background. The destruction of the two capital ships of Force Z was the IJNAF's outstanding accomplishment during the campaign. (Naval History and Heritage Command)

and arrange fighter cover. By 0800 hours on December 10, Phillips was located off Kuantan. An aircraft from *Prince of Wales* and a destroyer were sent to investigate and found no sign of the Japanese. After this, Phillips lingered for another 90 minutes off Kuantan to investigate another false report of some barges and a tug.

As Phillips chased phantoms instead of returning to the relative safety of Singapore, the Japanese set in motion an attack that changed naval history. Nine G3Ms from the Genzan Air Group took off at 0455 hours, followed by two C5M reconnaissance aircraft at 0530 hours. The main attack force of 85 G3M and G4M bombers took off between 0625 and 0800 hours. This force included the 26 Kanoya G4Ms, armed with torpedoes, and 59 G3Ms, 25 of which were armed with torpedoes, the rest with bombs.

The Japanese were not able to execute their doctrine of a coordinated attack. Instead, the battle developed into a series of smaller attacks conducted by groups of aircraft which were at the end of their fuel endurance. At 1013 hours, the Japanese spotted a destroyer which had been detached from Force Z because of fuel issues. Nine G3Ms attacked with bombs with no success. One of the reconnaissance aircraft spotted Force Z off Kuantan at 1015 hours. Even at this point, when Phillips knew he had been spotted and it was no longer necessary to maintain radio silence, he did not request fighter cover.

Just after 1100 hours, the Japanese attacks began to develop. The first group to attack was eight Mihoro G3Ms at 1115 hours against *Repulse*. Each bomber dropped two 550lb bombs, but only one hit the ship's hangar, causing a fire which was quickly dealt with. Against horizontal bombers flying a tight formation on a constant course and speed, British antiaircraft fire was fairly effective, with five of the eight bombers receiving damage.

The next attack by 17 torpedo-carrying G3Ms from the Genzan Air Group was the most critical of the battle. Eight bombers selected *Prince of Wales* for attack; the Japanese claimed three hits, but only two actually hit. These struck at 1144 hours on the port side abaft the rear 14in turret and buckled the outer propeller shaft, which flooded several compartments. The effects were dramatic – an 11.5-degree list, speed reduced to 15 knots, and no power for the main antiaircraft guns. The other nine G3Ms went after *Repulse* but the well-handled battlecruiser avoided them all. *Repulse* also avoided the bombs from six Mihoro G3Ms during this period.

From 1157 to 1202 hours, eight more Mihoro G3Ms attacked *Repulse* with torpedoes. Again, the ship's captain managed to avoid them all. Next to attack were the 26 G4Ms from the Kanoya Air Group from 1220 to 1232 hours. The Kanoya airmen confirmed their elite reputation by delivering a devastating attack. Six G4Ms attacked the crippled *Prince of Wales*, which was unable to maneuver. The ship was hit by four torpedoes on her starboard side which proved to be mortal. The other 20 bombers lined up for a pincer attack on *Repulse*. The maneuver was well executed and this time the battlecruiser's skillful captain could not avoid the barrage of weapons aimed at his ship. Five torpedoes hit the old battlecruiser which possessed minimal underwater protection. *Repulse* listed rapidly to port and sank at 1233 hours with the loss of 513 crewmen.

The fate of *Prince of Wales* was now all but certain. One Mihoro G3M placed a 1,100lb bomb on the upper deck, which penetrated to the main armored deck, where it exploded, causing heavy personnel casualties. With the ship's list to port increasing and with the ship settling, the order to abandon ship was given at 1315 hours. *Prince of Wales* heeled over to port five minutes later with 327 men.

The cost to the Japanese to cripple British sea power in the Far East was a mere three aircraft and 21 airmen lost and 27 other aircraft damaged. There were many reasons for the destruction of Force Z, but the main one is the most obvious. The IJNAF possessed an unsurpassed capability to attack maritime targets. Even if the British had managed to coordinate some fighter cover for Force Z (453 Squadron was standing by for that purpose), it would not have mattered. IJNAF training assumed heavy fighter defenses over enemy ships, and a handful of Buffalos would not have prevented the Japanese from pressing home their attacks with the same skill and determination.

Following the destruction of Force Z, most 22nd Air Flotilla operations were devoted to striking targets on Borneo, but periodic raids were directed at Singapore. By late December, the 22nd Air Flotilla had moved its fighter unit with 19 Zeros and 5 C5Ms to Kota Bharu and its bombers to Miri and Kuching on Borneo. On December 29, the Genzan Air Group returned to strike targets on Singapore. Eight G3Ms attacked Seletar Airfield, nine attacked Singapore city, and 14 bombed Keppel Harbor. On the first day of 1942, 25 G3Ms from the Mihoro Air Group attacked Seletar and Sembawang Airfields. Five 27 Squadron Blenheim IFs were sent up to intercept, but made no contact.

The air battle for Singapore heats up

The last seven weeks of the air campaign for Malaya and Singapore witnessed the final reduction of British air power. The IJAAF continued to stage its units forward to strike RAF facilities on Singapore and the 22nd Air Flotilla also continued to strike targets on Singapore. Concerted Japanese attacks on Singapore intensified on January 12 and continued until the British surrendered on February 15. During this period, the RAF averaged fewer than 30 fighters operational. All the bombers (an average of some 75) were moved to bases in Sumatra. Without sustained reinforcement or the means to adequately defend its few remaining bases, the RAF's final defeat was inevitable.

This is a Ki-43 of the 64th Sentai in late 1942 when the unit had moved to Ipoh in preparation for the final attack on Singapore. The aircraft has the markings of the 2nd Chutai. During the campaign, pilots from the 64th Sentai claimed 11 kills over Kuala Lumpur in Malaya, 39 over Singapore, and 18 over Java. (Andrew Thomas Collection)

RAF Reinforcements during the campaign:
51 crated Hurricanes and 24 pilots of 232 (Provisional) Squadron
18 Hudsons from 53 Squadron (only 15 arrived; the other three got as far as Burma)
48 Hurricanes from 232 and 258 Squadrons flown off carrier *Indomitable* for Batavia
24 Blenheim IVs from 84 Squadron (17 arrived on Sumatra)
24 Blenheim IVs from 211 Squadron (18 arrived on Sumatra)
18 Hudsons from 59 Squadron (7 arrived on Sumatra)
34 Hurricane pilots for 226 (Fighter) Group
British Antiaircraft Units
Singapore Island (some had forward-deployed batteries to a few airfields in Malaya)
1st Heavy Antiaircraft Regiment
2nd Heavy Antiaircraft Regiment
3rd Heavy Antiaircraft Regiment
3rd Light Antiaircraft Regiment
1st Antiaircraft Regiment (Indian Army)
5th Searchlight Regiment
Heavy antiaircraft regiments were equipped with 3-inch and 3.7-inch guns. The typical organization was three batteries of 12 guns but this varied by type and location.
Light antiaircraft regiments were equipped with 40-mm Bofors guns. A regiment typically was comprised of three batteries of 18 guns.
RAF Reserve Aircraft:
Blenheim I/IV 15
Buffalo 52
Hudson 7
Vildebeest 12
Catalina 2
Total 88
Singora
Patani
Khlaung Ngae
Sadao
Jitra
Alor Star
62 Sqn (11 x Blenheim I)
KEDDAH
27 Sqn (12 x Blenheim IF)
21 (RAAF) (12 x Buffalo)
Kroh
Betong
Sungei Patani
Ka Ketil
Butterworth
Penang
Sungei Bakap
Lubok Kiap
Malakoff
Grik
Port Weld
Taiping
Kuala Kangasar
Ipoh
Kampar
Stiawan
Tapah
Bidor
Telok Anson
Slim River
Tumpat
Kota Bharu
1 (RAAF) Sqn (12 x Hudson II)
36 Sqn (6 x Vildebeest)
100 Sqn (6 x Vildebeest)
Gong Kedak
Machang
Kuala Krai
Kuala Trengganu
KELANTAN
TRENGGANU
Kuala Dungun
Kuala Lipis
Jerantur
Raub
Bentong
Kuantan
60 Sqn (8 x Blenheim I)
8 (RAAF) Sqn (8 x Hudson II)
36 Sqn (6 x Vildebeest)
Maran
PAHANG
SELANGOR
Kuala Selangor
Kuala Lumpur
Port Swettenham
Morib
NEGRI
SEMBILAN
Seremban
Bahau
Gemas
Tampin
Port Dickson
Segamat
MALACCA
Malacca
Labis
JOHORE
Yong Peng
Muar
Batu Pahat
Ayer Hitam
Kluang
Rengani
Kahang
Jemaluang
Mersing
Endau
Kota Tinggi
Tebrau
Johore Bahru
Singapore
Occupied airfield
Unoccupied airfield
Landing ground
N
0
50 miles
50km
Sembawang
8 (RAAF) Sqn (4 x Hudson II)
453 (RAAF) Sqn (16 x Buffalo)
Seletar
100 Sqn (6 x Vildebeest)
205 Sqn (3 x Catalina)
Tengah
34 Sqn
(16 x Blenheim IV)
Kallang
243 (RNZAF) (16 x Buffalo)
488 Sqn (16 x Buffalo)
Singapore

OPPOSITE MAP OF MALAYA

The Japanese continued to move their air units forward as the RAF abandoned its bases in Malaya and fell back to Singapore. By December 27, the 3rd Air Division had moved some 80 aircraft to Sungei Patani. This was an attractive target for the RAF, which mounted a major raid on the airfield at dusk on the 27th. The attack was conducted by six Blenheims from 34 Squadron and five Hudsons of 8 RAAF Squadron. The strike caught the Japanese completely by surprise and proceeded to bomb and strafe uninterrupted for 30 minutes. Bomber crews claimed many aircraft hit, and a photo-reconnaissance Buffalo which flew over the base the following day confirmed the destruction of some 15 aircraft. Actual Japanese losses were heavy with eight to nine Ki-51s from the 27th Sentai destroyed and approximately 50 more aircraft damaged. Even this successful raid had little impact on the Japanese. Half of the damaged aircraft was quickly repaired and the 27th Sentai received seven Ki-51s from reserve stocks. On the night of December 28–29, 34 Squadron sent six more Blenheims to repeat the raid on Sungei Patani. The raid was not a success since only four bombers reached the target and they destroyed a single Ki-51. One Blenheim was hit by antiaircraft fire and was lost; a second was lost for operational reasons.

On January 1, Tengah Airfield on Singapore was attacked by a small number of Ki-48s and Ki-21s, and three Swordfish were destroyed. In return, the RAF kept up its counterair efforts against Japanese airfields. Three Blenheims were sent to attack the 98th Sentai's base; two were destroyed and a large number damaged. Kluang Airfield, the last fully operational RAF airfield in Malaya, came under attack from Ki-48s from the 75th and 90th Sentai escorted by Ki-43s on January 5. One Blenheim was destroyed on the ground.

By January 9, the 3rd Air Division moved the 64th Sentai with its Ki-43s to Ipoh Airfield. This did not escape the attention of the RAF, which ordered an immediate attack on the facility. Twelve Vildebeests of 36 Squadron were loaded with bombs for a night attack. Eleven bombers made it to the target and attacked; two Japanese fighters were destroyed. Only one of the biplanes was lost in the raid.

The following day, two 243 Squadron Buffalos made a radar-guided interception of a Ki-46 reconnaissance aircraft approaching Singapore and shot it down. This success did nothing to stop the Japanese ground advance. On January 11, they entered Kuala Lumpur. The British made some efforts to deny the airfield to the Japanese with demolitions. They estimated that it would take the Japanese three months to get the airfield operational; in fact, it took them three days.

The start of the Japanese air blitz on Singapore began on January 12. Both *sentai* of Ki-27s from the 12th Air Brigade had staged to Kuantan. Seventy-two of them were sent on a fighter sweep over Singapore. Eight Buffalos from 488 Squadron were ordered to intercept, and six more followed shortly. The Ki-27s used their superior maneuverability to gain an advantage. The 11th Sentai claimed ten Buffalos shot down. In fact, two were destroyed and five damaged out of the first eight sent to intercept. None of the second six was lost. Behind the Ki-27s was another group of 30 bombers escorted by 42 Ki-43s from the 59th and 64th Sentai. The Japanese suffered a major loss while taking off when four 59th Sentai fighters were lost in collisions. When this formation reached Singapore, only three Buffalos (two Dutch) were airborne; they managed to escape by using cloud cover. The bombing of Seletar Airfield accounted for a Hudson. In the afternoon, 70 Ki-27s returned and another major dogfight ensued. Again, the Buffalos were roughly handled with another two shot down and two more damaged. By the end of the day, the Singapore Fighter Command had proven it could not defend the island and the facilities on it. Out of 54 Buffalo sorties against the three Japanese formations, a total of six Buffalos were shot down, at least four damaged, and three more lost in accidents.

The RAF gamely continued to strike IJAAF airfields. At dawn on January 13, eight Hudsons hit Kuantan with uncertain results. On the same day, the IJNAF made a major daylight raid over Singapore after weather foiled its participation in the large strike the day before. A total of 81 bombers took off, but weather again made a shambles of Japanese plans. Three bombers hit Keppel Harbor at about 0930 hours. The Mihoro Air Group made for its alternative target and was attacked by eight Buffalos from 488 Squadron. The fighters attacked the bombers from the rear but the massed firepower of the bombers accounted for three Buffalos. To make things worse for 488 Squadron, the unit lost another fighter from operational causes.

In the afternoon of January 13, the two Ki-43 *sentai* made a fighter sweep over Singapore escorting a small group of bombers. 243 Squadron was able to intercept and shoot down one Ki-43. There was good news for the RAF though. A convoy arrived the same day with 51 crated Hurricanes and 24 pilots of the 232 (Provisional) Squadron. By January 17, 21 of the Hurricanes were ready for operations.

The Japanese kept up the pressure on January 14. Fifty-one IJNAF bombers were turned back by weather but the escorting Zeros met some 243 and 488 Squadron Buffalos. Later in the day, the Ki-27s returned. They encountered no RAF fighters, but did report an aircraft carrier in the harbor. Six more Blenheims were dispatched to strike Japanese aircraft on the ground at Sungei Patani. Two got through, but were unable to observe the results of their attack. One bomber failed to return.

Predictably, the report of an aircraft carrier in Keppel Harbor got the IJN very excited. To hit this valuable target, 27 G4Ms from the Kanoya Air Groups were dispatched on January 15 with a small escort of three Zeros. Arriving over the harbor at 0945 hours, they found no carrier and headed to Tengah to drop their bombs. This was just the beginning of the action since the IJAAF mounted several more raids during the day. Tengah and Sembawang were targeted by eight bombers each under the escort of 59th Sentai Ki-43s. Ki-27s also conducted patrols over the island and at least two Ki-44s from the 47th Independent Chutai made their first appearance over the island. The 64th Sentai escorted bombers to strike Seletar and Singapore City. Buffalos were up in strength during the day from 243, 488, and the combined 21/453 Squadrons; three Dutch Buffalos were also sent up. At least two RAF and one Dutch Buffalo were destroyed in air-to-air combat and many more damaged. In return, the Japanese lost at least one Ki-27 and one Ki-43.

Both sides mounted offensive operations on January 16. Twenty-four Genzan G3Ms, escorted by 12 Zeros, attacked Seletar Airfield in the morning. RAF Buffalos could not intercept and the bombers made an unmolested bomb run. Four bombers were damaged by antiaircraft fire. Later in the day, 243 Squadron Buffalos caught an IJN C5M reconnaissance aircraft and shot it down.

Throughout the day, the RAF made a concerted attempt to hit the main road in western Malaya following a reconnaissance report of heavy Japanese vehicle traffic. Six Dutch Martins and 12 Buffalos made the first attack. The fighters strafed until they were out of ammunition and reported good results. All the fighters returned, though five were hit by ground fire. The second strike was conducted by six more Buffalos and six Blenheims with anti-personnel bombs. One bomber was forced to crash-land when returning to Tengah. Notably, the RAF strikes were conducted in the complete absence of any Japanese fighters patrolling over their own lines of communications, another example of the 3rd Air Division's priorities. The RAF bomber force was reinforced when the first of three flights from the UK arrived in Singapore. Of the 18 Hudsons forming 53 Squadron, 15 arrived, the other three only getting as far as Burma.

Japanese pressure on Singapore intensified on January 17. Twelve Ki-21s bombed Singapore City in the morning, followed by 27 Ki-48s attacking Tengah Airfield escorted by Ki-43s. For the first time, Sembawang Airfield was hit by bombers. The raid was conducted by 24 G3Ms from the Mihoro Air Group. The bombing was very accurate, destroying three Buffalos and three Hudsons; three Buffalos and three Hudsons were also damaged. Airfield facilities were also badly damaged and the raid induced all the local labor to flee, thus forcing the RAF base personnel to assume all support functions. While the IJN bombers hit Sembawang, eight escorting Zeros strafed Tengah and accounted for three Blenheim IVs damaged. Three Dutch Buffalos were sent up to intercept the bombers, followed by all available fighters from 243 Squadron. One of the Dutch fighters was shot down by the bombers' defensive fire, but the Buffalos claimed several bombers downed.

Three of the five IJNAF bomber units involved in the campaign were equipped with the Mitsubishi G3M medium bomber. Able to carry both bombs and torpedoes, the G3M was able to strike both land and maritime targets. (Naval History and Heritage Command)

More IJAAF aircraft arrived over the island late in the morning. Ki-21s from the 60th Sentai bombed Far East Forces Headquarters while the escorting Ki-43s went after flying boats moored in Seletar. Two Catalinas were destroyed and another two damaged.

Raids against Singapore resumed before noon on the 18th. The first was conducted by 26 Kanoya G4Ms, escorted by 11 Zeros and 2 C5Ms. Buffalos from 243 and 488 Squadrons rose to intercept. For the first and only time of the campaign, the Buffalos found themselves with a height advantage over the Zeros. They conducted a head-on diving attack which accounted for two Zeros. One Buffalo was badly damaged and written off upon landing. The IJAAF followed up two hours later with a raid composed of Ki-21s escorted by Ki-43s. Ki-27s and Ki-44s also reported engaging Buffalos. Twelve Buffalos were sent to intercept but were caught still climbing when attacked by the Japanese. Two were shot down and five damaged. With the Buffalo force dwindling, the Hurricanes of 232 (Provisional) Squadron assumed primary responsibility for defending the island with 21 operational aircraft. The five surviving Dutch Buffalos were withdrawn to Java.

The following day, Singapore was spared attack as both sides devoted many sorties to supporting the ground battle. A RAF reconnaissance flight over Kuala Lumpur sighted many Japanese fighters present. A night strike by nine Vildebeests damaged only a single Japanese transport aircraft.

Given a day's respite, the Japanese were able to mount a major raid on Singapore on January 20. The IJNAF committed 26 Mihoro G3Ms and 18 Genzan G3Ms escorted by 18 Zeros and two C5Ms. The IJAAF committed Ki-21s from the 12th and 60th Sentai escorted by Ki-43s from the 64th Sentai. This day marked the combat debut of the Hurricanes. Twelve of the fighters were sent up to intercept. Despite the fact that most of the Hurricane pilots were inexperienced, they held their own. Three Ki-43s were downed, as were three Hurricanes. The Hurricanes were able to jump a group of Ki-21s and claimed several, though none was actually lost. Seven Buffalos were also sent aloft, but failed to make contact. The RAF continued efforts to strike Japanese airfields. After dusk, seven Blenheims from

34 Squadron hit Kuala Lumpur, claiming many aircraft hit. One Blenheim was lost to Ki-43s. That night, seven Vildebeests also struck the airfield. Eight Hudsons from 8 RAAF Squadron hit Kuantan with no result.

The IJNAF returned to Singapore on January 21 in strength with 25 Mihoro G3Ms and 27 Kanoya G4Ms escorted by nine Zeros. Only two Hurricanes made contact with the Mihoro bombers. In a beam attack, they hit one G3M and watched its bomb load explode, which apparently also accounted for the two nearest bombers. In fact, only one bomber was lost. The bombers went on to bomb Tengah where they caught several RAF bombers on the ground. Two Hudsons and two Blenheims were destroyed, and a third Blenheim was damaged. Hurricanes also intercepted a large IJAAF strike and engaged Ki-43s from the 64th Sentai. Two Hurricanes were lost and a third damaged.

More intense action continued over Singapore on the 22nd. Twenty-five Genzan G3Ms, 27 Kanoya G4Ms, nine Zeros, and two C5Ms arrived over their targets in the late morning. The Genzan bombers attacked Kallang and destroyed one of four Buffalos as they were taking off. Two more Buffalos were destroyed by shrapnel. At least eight Hurricanes were already airborne and these conducted a diving attack on the formation of G3Ms. One bomber was destroyed, another forced to ditch on the way home, and one more force-landed. The escorting Zeros hit back hard, shooting down five Hurricanes and damaging one. Two Zeros were also lost. The Kanoya G4Ms attacked Sembawang and claimed 15 aircraft destroyed. In fact, two Martins were destroyed, while two more Martins and four Hudsons were damaged.

The attrition to the RAF fighter force continued the next day. Hurricanes engaged the daily raid and tangled with Ki-43s escorting 27 Ki-21s. The bombers delivered their payloads at Seletar, destroying three aircraft and damaging seven. Three Hurricanes

The IJAAF still flew the dated Mitsubishi Ki-30 light bomber in both the 27th and 31st Sentai during the campaign. It had little to recommend for it except for an ease of maintenance since it was extremely vulnerable to fighter interception. It epitomizes the largely obsolescent aircraft that the IJAAF went to war with, the principal exception being the Ki-43. (Philip Jarrett Collection)

were lost tangling with the Ki-43s. The relentless bombing of the four airfields on Singapore forced the RAF to pull all remaining Hudsons and Blenheims back to bases on Sumatra. 243 and 488 Squadrons were down to a total of two operational Buffalos. Some reinforcement was received on a convoy arriving on January 24, but only in the form of inexperienced pilots.

On January 26, a major air-sea battle developed which fully displayed the RAF's limited capabilities to perform one of its primary missions – to successfully attack a Japanese seaborne invasion. A Japanese convoy was spotted at 0745 hours on January 26 just 20 miles northeast of Endau, a small port on the southeastern coast of Malaya. The convoy was composed of the transports *Kanberra Maru* and *Kansai Maru*, escorted by a light cruiser, seven destroyers, and five large minesweepers. The British believed this was a troop or supply convoy moving south to support the final Japanese attack on Singapore. In fact, the transports were carrying elements of an IJAAF ground support battalion with aviation fuel, bombs, and stores. In any event, this convoy could not be allowed to arrive at Endau and an all-out effort was ordered. The only strike aircraft immediately available were 12 Vildebeest torpedo bombers and nine Hudsons from two RAAF squadrons. The crews of 36 and 100 Squadrons had been promised that they would not be asked to fly their slow biplanes on daytime missions, but the perceived desperation of the situation forced them into the air during the day against a heavily defended target. The first attack was planned for the early afternoon after the aircraft could be fueled and armed from the previous night's operations.

The 12 Vildebeests headed toward the Japanese fleet at 1,000ft at their cruising speed of 90 knots escorted by six Buffalos. The aircraft were loaded with bombs since torpedoes were thought to be useless in the shallow water where the transports were anchored. Behind the ancient Vildebeests were the nine Hudsons escorted by six Buffalos and nine Hurricanes. The Japanese were expecting an attack on a convoy landing so close to Singapore. From the 1st and 11th Sentai, 18 Ki-27s were flying protective cover with one pre-production Ki-44 from the 47th Independent Fighter Chutai.

The approaching Vildebeests were hit first by 11th Sentai and then by 1st Sentai Ki-27s. The slow biplanes and their escorts were relentlessly attacked in a series of dogfights. Japanese claims of 11 shot down, three probables and three Vildebeests forced to crash-land were another case of over-claiming, but not by much. In exchange, one Ki-27 was shot down and another damaged. The British pilots who bravely pressed home their attacks did score several hits on *Kanberra Maru*.

A second strike was hastily dispatched in the wake of the first. This one consisted of nine Vildebeests, three Albacores all with bombs with an escort of seven Hurricanes, and the last four serviceable Buffalos. The fighters took off late, which put the biplanes over the target at about 1730 hours with no cloud cover and no escorts. Ten Ki-27s from the 1st Sentai intercepted together with two Ki-44s. Again, RAF losses were heavy and damage to the transports minor. The last strike of the day was made by six Hudsons from 62 Squadron with no escorts. The bombers attacked at low level and then were chased down by Ki-27s; two Hudsons were lost.

This supreme RAF effort was assessed to be successful by the British. Both transports were reported hit by the brave air crews and as many as 13 Japanese fighters were claimed to have been shot down. In reality, the operation was nothing more than a suicide run by the biplanes from 36 and 100 Squadrons. Total losses were ten Vildebeests, two Albacores, two Hudsons, and one Hurricane. Two more Vildebeests crash-landed and were written off. Both of the commanding officers from the two Vildebeest squadrons were lost, as were another 30 aircrew killed, eight wounded, and two taken prisoner. The result of this sacrifice was minimal. *Kanberra Maru* took several hits but survived and only lost eight dead. *Kansai Maru* suffered only minor damage.

The fall of Singapore

As the IJAAF positioned itself for the final attack on Singapore it mustered some 170 aircraft. Among these were 30 Ki-21 based near Sungei Patani, 20 Ki-48s based at Ipoh, 20 Ki-51s based at Kuala Lumpur and Kluang, and 80 fighters (1st and 11th Sentai with Ki-27s at Kuantun, the 64th Sentai at Ipoh, and the 59th Sentai at Kuala Lumpur, both with Ki-43s). Fighter losses to date had been fairly heavy – 32 Ki-27s and 23 Ki-43s – but only 60 percent were due to enemy action. Many of those were destroyed on the ground, not in aerial combat.

The final two weeks of the Singapore air campaign were anticlimactic. The Japanese kept up the pressure against the RAF airfields on the island with both IJAAF and IJNAF units. British air defense operations, though reinforced by the arrival of the Hurricanes, grew progressively weaker until during the final week of the campaign there were only sporadic attempts to intercept the daily Japanese raids over Singapore. The constant battering that Singapore was subjected to from the air was a prime factor in the declining morale of the defenders and severely undermined the will of the British garrison to continue the fight. Added to the increasing civilian death toll, there was a growing sense that the campaign was drawing to an end.

On January 27, the Kanoya Air Group delivered a stinging attack on Kallang when bombs destroyed two Hurricanes, heavily damaged three more, and inflicted light damage on a further three. Almost all of 243 Squadron's Buffalos were destroyed and damaged. Damage to the airfield's infrastructure was also heavy, and two Blenheims were destroyed. After the attack, the last aircraft from 243 Squadron were given to 453 Squadron and the squadron was disbanded. The remnants of 21 RAAF Squadron were embarked on a ship and sent home. Only one Buffalo squadron remained on the island. The Hurricane force received a large boost when 48 aircraft from 232 and 258 Squadrons were flown off the carrier *Indomitable* to Batavia on Java. These were subsequently sent north to bases on Sumatra and Singapore. Of the 51 crated Hurricanes which had arrived earlier, only 25 were operational or in short-term repair; 17 had already been lost, with another nine in long-term repair. On the same day, Seletar was attacked by 26 G3Ms from Genzan Air Group escorted by 18 Zeros and a C5M on the 29th. Sembawang was attacked by IJAAF units and intercepted by a section of Hurricanes and Buffalos.

There were four airfields on Singapore. This photograph shows the effect of a Japanese bombing raid on Kallang, which was the southernmost airfield and the last to be evacuated by the RAF before the surrender of the island's garrison. (Australian War Memorial)

The newly arrived Hurricanes were quickly attrited in continuous action against the Japanese. This is the aircraft of Flight Lieutenant Wright, commander of 232 Squadron, who was forced to crash-land his aircraft at Kallang after engaging Ki-21s and then Ki43s on February 7. Wright survived the crash. (Andrew Thomas Collection)

On January 31, the last British troops crossed from Johore onto Singapore. Within four days, the Japanese had closed up to the strait and began an artillery bombardment of the British defenses. At 2000 hours on February 8, two Japanese divisions attacked across the strait and gained a foothold. A planned British counterattack failed to materialize. On the 10th, the British withdrew from the best defensive positions outside Singapore city. The final collapse was only days away. Percival decided to surrender on February 15.

To support the impending attack across the strait, the Japanese stepped up the pressure on Singapore with daily bombings. On January 31, IJAAF bombers appeared over the island escorted by Ki-43s. Seven Hurricanes from 258 Squadron were launched to intercept, joined by some additional aircraft from 232 Provisional Squadron. In the first engagement for 258 Squadron, the Japanese prevailed. One Ki-43 was shot down and the Hurricanes got a shot at the bombers, claiming several. British losses were high with one Hurricane shot down and three more forced to crash-land, making them effectively lost.

By this point, the airfields on Singapore were being subjected to Japanese shell fire. It was decided that only the six surviving Buffalos together with eight Hurricanes would remain at Tengah and all other operational aircraft were ordered to withdraw to Palembang on Sumatra. The 13 surviving Vildebeests were ordered to Java along with the last Catalinas from 205 Squadron.

The daily raid on February 1 by Ki-21 bombers escorted by Ki-43s was intercepted by four Buffalos; two were shot down. The following two days saw Japanese bombers hit multiple targets with no opposition. On February 4, the RAF planned a large strike on Kluang Airfield escorted by 12 Hurricanes from 258 Squadron staging from Tengah. The ground crews at Tengah could not prepare the fighters in time, so they did not participate. The Blenheim bombers ended up striking a rail line near Kluang, and the Hudsons proceeded to the airfield, where one was shot down by Ki-43s.

On February 5, Tengah was evacuated in favor of Kallang. The Japanese attacked Kallang the same day without fighter opposition. In response, the RAF ordered all flyable aircraft to Palembang – nine Buffalos, four Hudsons, and 13 Hurricanes. Hurricanes from Palembang patrolled over the island and accounted for two Ki-27s from the 1st Sentai shot down on

4 February Attack
Group 1 – 27 Kanoya Air Group G4M1s
Group 2 – 9 Takao Air Group G4M1s
Group 3 – 24 1st Air Group G3Ms
15 February Attack
Group 1 – 30 Ryujo B5N1/2s
Group 2 – 23 Genzan Air Group G3Ms
Group 3 – 27 Mihoro Air Group G3Ms
Group 4 – 17 Kanoya Air Group G4M1s
THAILAND
INDOCHINA
Saigon
Cam Ranh Bay
South China Sea
Luzon
Clark Field
Manila
Cavite
Bataan Peninsula
Manila Bay
Corregidor
Legaspi
PHILIPPINES
Panay
Sulu Sea
Del Monte
Davao
Jolo
Singora
Kota Bharu
Penang
Sabang
MALAY STATES
Kuantan
Endau
Singapore
Medan
Pakanberu
NORTH BORNEO
BRUNEI
Miri
SARAWAK
Tarakan
Celebes Sea
Menado
Kema
Halmahera
Kuching
Singkawang
Samarinda
NETHERLANDS EAST INDIES
Balikpapan
Borneo
MOLUCCAS
NEW GUINEA
Babo
Bangka Strait
Sumatra
Bangka Island
CSF
Palembang
Palembang 2
Gaspar Strait
Java Sea
Banjarmasin
Makassar Strait
Celebes
Kendari
Ambon
Makassar
Banda Sea
Bantam Bay
Tandjong Priok
Tjikampek
Sunda Strait
Tjisaoek
Kalidjati
Kemajoran
Semplak
Andir
Java
Tjilatjap
Bawean Island
Madoera
Blimbing
Surabaja
Madoien
Malang
CSF
Denpesar
Bali
Flores Sea
Lombok
Bali Strait
Badoeng Strait
Lombok Strait
Dili
Timor
Koepang
Arafura Sea
INDIAN OCEAN
Christmas Island
Melville Island
Bathurst Island
Darwin
Timor Sea
AUSTRALIA
N
0
500 miles
0
500km

OPPOSITE IJNAF ATTACKS ON THE ABDA COMBINED STRIKING FORCE ON FEBRUARY 4 AND 15

February 6. The next day, Hurricane patrols encountered large bombing raids over Singapore. On this day, two Hurricanes were lost.

On February 8, the day of the Japanese attack across the Johore Strait, the IJNAF concentrated on attacking the many ships evacuating personnel from Singapore. Concurrently, the IJAAF made a major effort with 102 bomber sorties and 75 Ki-27 sorties. Eight Hurricanes were on patrol but could not catch the bombers after they dropped their loads on Kallang. After noon, ten Hurricanes mounted another patrol. In combat with Ki-43s, three more Hurricanes were badly damaged.

With Japanese ground forces firmly established on Singapore on February 9, the IJAAF mounted continuous sorties over the front lines. Hurricanes attacked some of these and, using a height advantage, claimed several Japanese aircraft. 232 Squadron had been using Kallang as a staging base, but now the base was ordered to be evacuated. Eight Hurricanes departed for Palembang at first light on the 10th, and three more were made flyable and departed the following day. The air battle for Malaya and Singapore was over.

The air campaign for the NEI

The Japanese campaign to occupy the NEI was a complex and rapid operation. To provide the most clarity in the space available, the operations will be covered along the main avenues of advance instead of on a chronological basis. Initial operations (Phase 1 to the Japanese) were focused on Borneo, supported by the 22nd Air Flotilla. Phase 2 opened on December 26 when the 21st and 23rd Air Flotillas led the attack into central and eastern NEI. The Japanese operation unfolded in a series of invasions at almost breakneck speed, but never out of the range of seaborne or land-based air cover. Even before the fall of Singapore, the IJAAF was attacking Allied air bases on Sumatra. The two principal Allied air bases on the southern end of the island were seized in mid-February, which allowed the IJAAF to move

The mainstay aircraft of the MLD was the German-designed Do 24K. This was a robust aircraft with a top speed of 210mph. It was armed only with two machine guns and one 20mm cannon, so it was unable to defend itself against fighter attack. In the early part of the campaign, the Dutch used it for strike missions until losses became prohibitive. Only six aircraft survived the campaign. (Netherlands Institute for Military History)

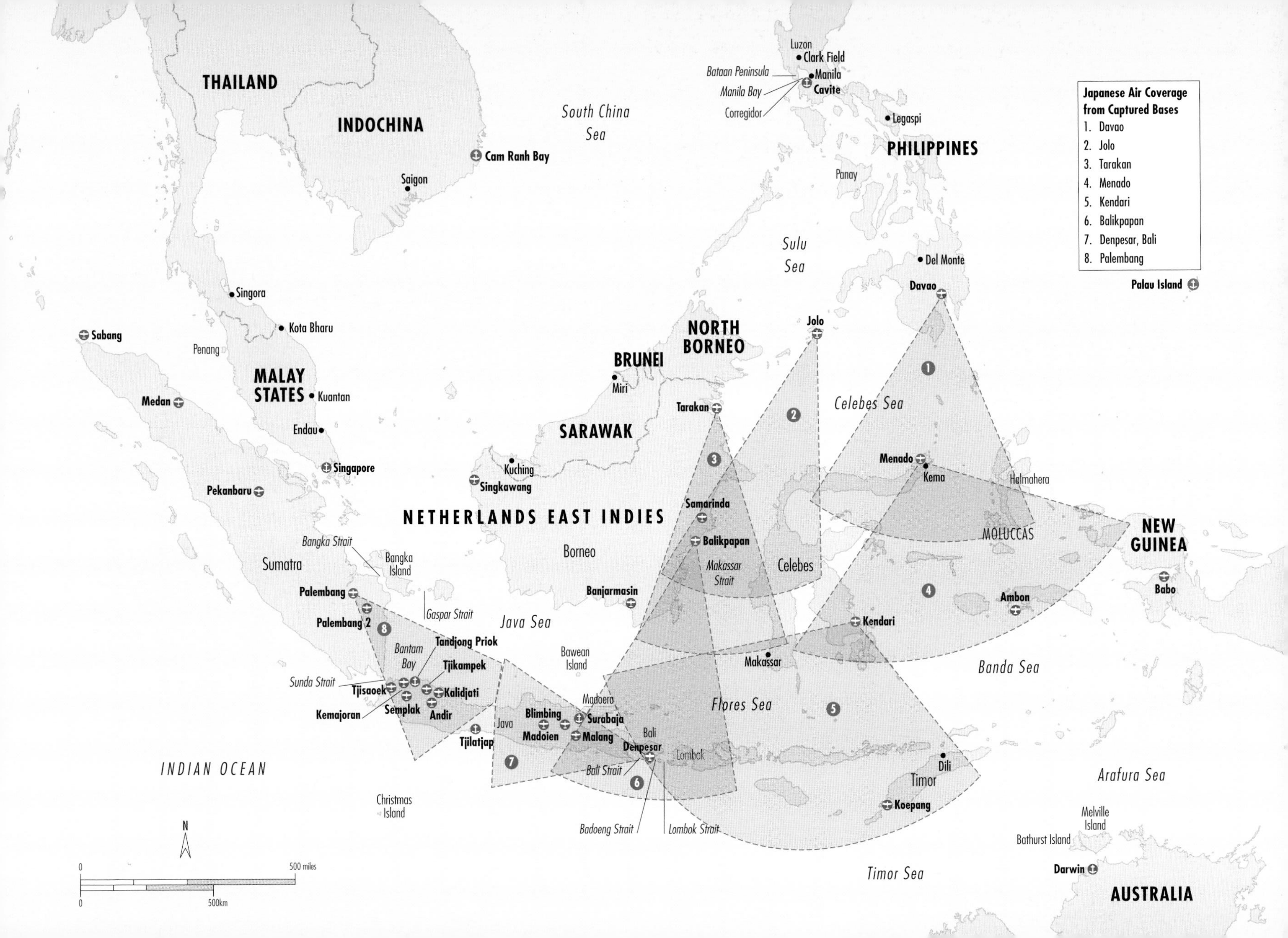

Japanese Air Coverage from Captured Bases
1. Davao
2. Jolo
3. Tarakan
4. Menado
5. Kendari
6. Balikpapan
7. Denpesar, Bali
8. Palembang
THAILAND
INDOCHINA
PHILIPPINES
MALAY STATES
BRUNEI
NORTH BORNEO
SARAWAK
NETHERLANDS EAST INDIES
NEW GUINEA
AUSTRALIA
South China Sea
Sulu Sea
Celebes Sea
Java Sea
Flores Sea
Banda Sea
Arafura Sea
Timor Sea
INDIAN OCEAN
Luzon
Clark Field
Manila
Cavite
Bataan Peninsula
Manila Bay
Corregidor
Legaspi
Panay
Del Monte
Davao
Palau Island
Cam Ranh Bay
Saigon
Singora
Kota Bharu
Penang
Kuantan
Endau
Singapore
Sabang
Medan
Pekanbaru
Jolo
Miri
Tarakan
Kuching
Singkawang
Menado
Kema
Halmahera
MOLUCCAS
Samarinda
Balikpapan
Makassar Strait
Celebes
Borneo
Sumatra
Bangka Strait
Bangka Island
Gaspar Strait
Palembang
Palembang 2
Banjarmasin
Ambon
Babo
Kendari
Makassar
Bantam Bay
Tandjong Priok
Tjikampek
Kalidjati
Andir
Semplak
Tjisaoek
Kemajoran
Sunda Strait
Bawean Island
Madoera
Surabaja
Blimbing
Madoien
Malang
Java
Tjilatjap
Bali
Denpesar
Lombok
Bali Strait
Badoeng Strait
Lombok Strait
Dili
Timor
Koepang
Christmas Island
Melville Island
Bathurst Island
Darwin
N
0
500 miles
500km

OPPOSITE JAPANESE AIR COVERAGE FROM CAPTURED AIRFIELDS IN THE NEI

forward and begin a counterair operation on Allied air forces in western Java. Concurrently, the IJNAF was neutralizing Allied air power in eastern Java and cutting the air reinforcement links between Australia and Java. Phase 3 of the campaign was the landings on Java. At all points of the campaign, Allied air forces fought bravely and aggressively, but were only able to impose a brief delay on the Japanese timetable.

The invasion of Borneo

On December 16, a Dutch flying boat spotted the Japanese landing at Miri on British Borneo. The following day the Dutch reacted aggressively with several air strikes. A Do 24 bombed a Japanese transport without success and was shot down by an F1M from *Kamikawa Maru*. Six Martins followed but were unsuccessful due to bad weather. The same F1M claimed a bomber but all escaped. Two more Do 24s attacked next. One claimed to have damaged a transport, but the other scored the MLD's biggest success of the campaign when flying boat X-32 of GVT-7 dropped five bombs on destroyer *Shinonome*, scoring three direct hits and one near miss. The aft magazine detonated and the ship sank in minutes with no survivors from a crew of 221. In almost all cases during the NEI campaign, the Dutch responded immediately to Japanese invasions, but they were never successful in stopping or significantly impeding Japanese advances. There were two main reasons for this. Japanese amphibious doctrine called for landings at night, meaning that when the Dutch aircraft showed up the next morning, the landing force was already ashore. Given the weakness of Dutch ground forces, this meant that the landing was invariably successful. Secondly, follow-up air attacks on the invasion force were mounted piecemeal and the ML-KNIL demonstrated little ability to hit maritime targets.

The Japanese expanded operations against Allied facilities on Borneo. On December 18, 26 Mihoro G3Ms attacked shipping off Kuching, claiming one ship sunk. The next day, Kuching town was hit by 18 Genzan G3Ms. Nine Mihoro G3Ms raided Pontianak Airfield in western Borneo. This raid was intercepted by three Dutch Buffalos. One G3M was forced to ditch on the way back to Saigon. Also on December 19, six Martins from bases at Singkawang and Samarinda went after Japanese shipping off Miri. No hits were made in the bad weather conditions and F1Ms from *Kamikawa Maru* knocked down one bomber.

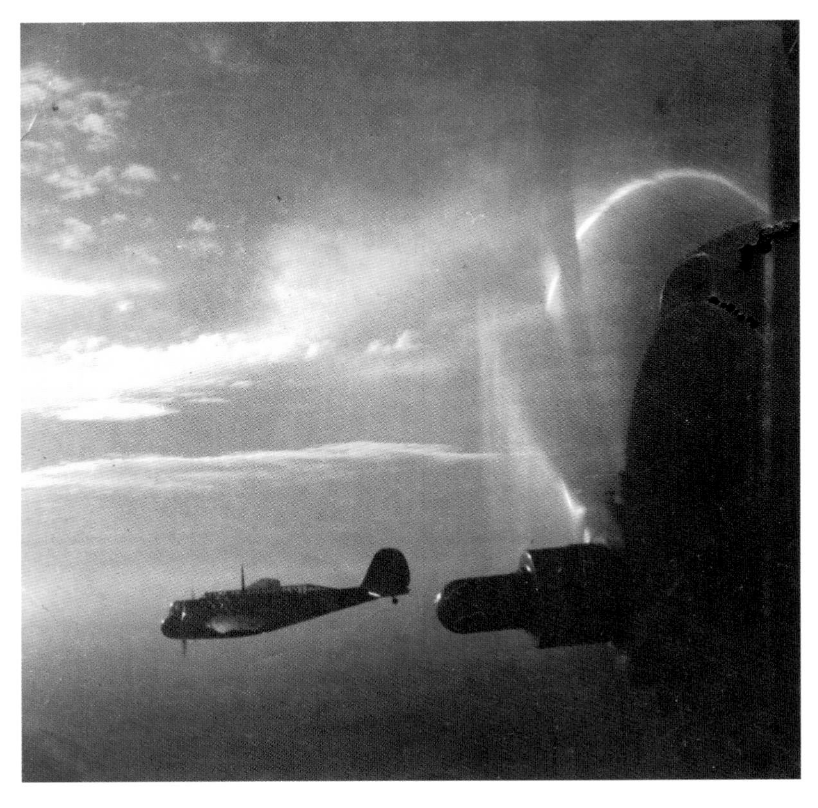

This photo shows the Dutch strike of Glenn Martin bombers on December 26 against Japanese shipping at Kuching. The three bombers attacked without fighter opposition and on this occasion bombed accurately. A Japanese transport and a fleet minesweeper were sunk – the most successful Dutch air strike of the campaign. (Netherlands Institute for Military History)

The Dutch mounted another attack on December 20 against Japanese shipping off Miri. Six Martins comprised the raid with two Buffalo escorts to contend with the F1Ms. The Buffalos claimed one F1M, but it was only damaged. Again, no hits were scored by the bombers. In response, 26 Kanoya G4Ms hit targets in western Borneo including Singkawang Airfield. On December 22, the Japanese moved 15 Zeros and a C5M to Miri, which were joined by nine Mihoro G3Ms. Twenty-four Mihoro G3Ms bombed Singkawang Airfield and destroyed two Martins being readied for an attack.

On December 23, the Dutch spotted a six-ship convoy headed from Miri to Kuching under heavy escort. The convoy was covered by Zeros from Miri and *Kamikawa Maru* F1Ms. The floatplanes engaged shadowing Dutch Do 24s; one was damaged, but an F1M was badly damaged and sank after it landed. Five Blenheim IVs from 34 Squadron and three 8 RAAF Squadron Hudsons attacked the convoy with no success. The convoy survived air and submarine attacks to land troops on Sarawak, which fell without a fight.

The following day, 18 Kanoya G4Ms and seven Mihoro G3Ms, escorted by six Zeros, launched a major raid to neutralize Singkawang. Bad weather prevented the bombers from attacking, but the Zeros strafed and destroyed one Martin. Two days later, Tarakan in northeast Borneo was subjected to its first attack. Seven Mihoro G3Ms bombed the airfield and claimed an aircraft destroyed on the ground. Dutch Martin bombers returned to attack the shipping off Kuching; they got through unhindered and sank an auxiliary transport and the 620-ton minesweeper *W-6*.

The central NEI offensive

Japanese troops landed at Davao on Mindanao on December 20. This provided a base for the advance into the central NEI. The IJNAF committed the Kanoya and 1st Air Groups from the 21st Air Flotilla and the 3rd Air Group was detached from the 23rd Air Flotilla.

Aware of the importance of Davao as a staging base, the Dutch attacked it on December 23 to prevent its use by the Japanese. Six Do 24s made the attack and sank a tanker. F1Ms forced one of the Do 24s to ditch, but another flying boat set down to save the crew.

The MLD was in the process of replacing its Do 24Ks with American-built Catalinas when the war began. The Dutch used the Catalina to complement the Do 24K during the campaign, but the Catalina was also subjected to heavy losses when used on strike missions. The MLD's flying boats performed generally well in their primary mission of maritime patrol, giving forewarning of major Japanese advances. (Netherlands Institute for Military History)

The Japanese seized Jolo in the Sulu Archipelago on December 25 and immediately moved fighters from the 3rd Air Group into the island's airfield. The following day, six Zeros led by a C5M conducted a morning sweep over Menado in the northern Celebes. They found four Do 24s from the Davao raid in a nearby lake and proceeded to destroy them all by strafing.

The MLD's flying boat force was reinforced when the USN's Patrol Wing Ten moved to Java from the Philippines. The newly arrived Catalinas' first mission was against Japanese shipping at Jolo on December 27. Using the lumbering Catalinas in a maritime strike role was possible only in the absence of enemy fighters. The day before, Tainan Air Group Zeros had staged to Jolo and they gave the six Catalinas a hot reception. Four were shot down and no Zeros were lost.

The next day, seven Zeros led by a C5M flew from Davao to strike Tarakan. They were intercepted by Dutch Buffalos. For the cost of a single Zero damaged, the Japanese made short work of the Buffalos, shooting down three and forcing another to crash-land. The 3rd Air Group Zeros were followed by seven Mihoro Air Group G3Ms escorted by four Zeros from Miri. Three Dutch Martins attempted to hit the Japanese airfield at Miri; five Zeros intercepted the raiders and in an extended chase shot down one, forced another to ditch, and placed over 300 bullet holes in the only bomber that survived.

The Dutch received a much-needed reinforcement when the first USAAF bombers arrived in Java in late December. Much was expected from these long-range aircraft which were believed to be able to deliver accurate attacks against maritime targets. The first B-17 raid was conducted by eight bombers against shipping at Davao on January 4. On this occasion, the B-17s lived up to their hype by damaging the heavy cruiser *Myoko*.

On January 6, the IJNAF expanded operations into the eastern NEI. Twenty-four Kanoya G4Ms and six H6K flying boats set out from Davao to raid Ambon Island. Only three H6Ks and 14 G4Ms found the target, which was an airfield. The attack caught the defenders completely by surprise but damage was minimal.

A major invasion convoy coming from Davao bound for Tarakan with 14 heavily escorted transports was spotted by USN Catalinas on January 10. It was attacked by three B-17s and three Dutch Martins without effect. F1Ms from *Sanyo Maru* shot down one Martin.

The pace of the Japanese advance accelerated on January 11. Japanese troops landed at Tarakan and the defenders were quickly forced to surrender on the following day. The Japanese invasion force offshore braced for Allied air attacks. Dutch Martins at Saraminda Airfield located on the central coast of eastern Borneo were reinforced by two more Martin squadrons. Bad weather kept these aircraft on the ground until afternoon. After finally getting airborne, they proceeded to hit the invasion force off Tarakan and claimed several hits. Two Martins were lost when they crash-landed. Three of seven USAAF B-17s staging from Kendari were able to get through to the target and fought off intercepting Zeros, forcing one to crash-land. The weather was too bad for the big bombers to drop bombs.

On January 11, another Japanese invasion force landed on Menado on the northeast tip of the Celebes. The invasion was covered by seaplane carriers *Chitose* and *Mizuho*. The F1Ms from these ships put up a strong defense against seven attacking Catalinas (three Dutch, four USN). Two were shot down (one Dutch, one USN) and the other two Dutch aircraft were damaged. Four RAAF Hudsons from Ambon were also intercepted but shot down one floatplane and damaged two more so severely that they sank upon landing. The Australians claimed hits on three ships, but only one was near-missed. Augmenting the seaborne invasion was an airborne drop. Twenty-eight G3Ms from the 1st Air Group dropped 324 paratroopers over the airfield, which was quickly captured. The following day ten Zeros and a C5M from the 3rd Air Group moved into the airfield. These fighters shattered a raid by RAAF Hudsons flying from Ambon to hit the shipping off Menado on January 12. Seven Zeros intercepted the first group of five Hudsons and quickly shot down four. Another group of three got through unmolested and dropped their bombs with no success.

Another of the forgotten Japanese aircraft of the campaign was the Mitsubishi Ki-15 reconnaissance aircraft. The same aircraft was known as the C5M in IJNAF service; one is shown here. By the start of the war it was obsolescent and lacked the speed to avoid fighter interception. In IJNAF service it still provided valuable service as a guide aircraft for Zeros performing long-range over-water missions and for bomb damage assessment using its onboard cameras. (Philip Jarrett Collection)

The Dutch made a major effort to strike shipping off Tarakan on January 13. Five flights of Martins from Samarinda were committed but ran into Tinian Air Group Zeros. The Zeros made short work of the unescorted bombers with as many as seven being shot down.

The Japanese tried again to neutralize Ambon Airfield on January 15. Eighteen Zeros from the 3rd Air Group were sent to strafe the airfield led by a C5M. Two Dutch Buffalos were scrambled but both were quickly shot down. Following the fighters were 26 Kanoya G4Ms which delivered an accurate attack on the airfield. The seven operational Hudsons based at Ambon were in the air so avoided destruction. Two USN Catalinas at a nearby seaplane base were destroyed by strafing. The next morning, four Zeros led by a C5M returned and claimed a flying boat destroyed on the ground. Another USN PBY was engaged in the air, but the waist gunner reported hitting a Zero and setting it on fire.

The next two strikes were conducted by USAAF bombers. On January 17, three LB-30 and two B-17 bombers from Java staged through Kendari to attack Menado. The morning strike encountered large numbers of Zeros from the 3rd Air Group. The two B-17s were damaged but returned to Kendari. The Japanese dispatched three Zeros to catch the bombers on the ground at Kendari. One got away, but the other was heavily damaged and never flew again. The LB-30s were also roughly handled, two being forced to crash-land by the Zeros. The next raid, on January 19, was composed of nine B-17s which struck a convoy near Jolo; only six of the bombers actually attacked on account of the weather conditions. The Americans claimed two ships hit, but as usual they missed.

On January 20, four Zeros led by a C5M from the Tainan Air Group conducted the first Japanese strike on Bandjermasin in southern Borneo. They caught a Dutch Catalina in the water and set it afire. This was a precursor to the next major Japanese move. On January 21, a large Japanese invasion fleet was spotted in the Makassar Strait bound for Balikpapan. On the afternoon of the 23rd, two Martins and 20 Buffalos with small bombs attacked the convoy. Four of the transports were hit and one was set afire and later sank. One Buffalo was lost. Early on the 24th, the Japanese landed at Balikpapan. This prompted a major Allied effort to strike the invasion force when daylight came. Nine Martins, six B-17Es, and two B-17Ds took part in the raids. The bombers claimed hits on several transports, but only *Nana Maru* was sunk by the Martins. Tainan Air Group Zeros tenaciously attacked the B-17s and claimed three; in fact only three were slightly damaged and were able to return to Java. Action was also heavy over Samarinda Airfield which was now bypassed by the Japanese landing at Balikpapan. One Zero was shot down by antiaircraft fire in the morning. In the afternoon, six more Zeros returned and were intercepted by Buffalos. Two were shot down by the Japanese in exchange for one Zero. When a flight of three Martins showed up to land, all three were set upon by Zeros and destroyed.

The 24th saw another major Japanese advance. An invasion force of six transports, heavily escorted, delivered Japanese naval troops to Kendari. The invasion was covered by seaplane carriers *Chitose* and *Mizuho*, but there was no Allied air opposition. This was one of the most important developments of the campaign. Kendari was one of the largest airfields in the NEI and it fell into Japanese hands intact. Possession of Kendari brought eastern Java and Timor Island, which was an important link in the air reinforcement route from Australia to Java, into range of Japanese air attack. The Japanese quickly moved to exploit this position. The 21st Air Flotilla with 35 Zeros of the 3rd Air Group and bombers of the 1st Air Group moved to Kendari. On January 27, the 23rd Air Flotilla began moving to Balikpapan. Balikpapan proved unsuitable for the large G3Ms and these later moved to Kendari. Tinian Air Group Zeros continued to operate from Balikpapan.

With Balikpapan lost, the Dutch decided to withdraw their vulnerable bombers from Samarinda. On January 25, ten operational Martins set off to attack shipping at Balikpapan and then fly on to Java. Weather split the formation up and they were attacked by Zeros before reaching their target. One was shot down, and three more were forced to make emergency landings. Five bombers reached Makassar still under attack; one Zero was shot down by return fire. On the same day, B-17s returned to Balikpapan. Zeros attacked a formation of seven and claimed none. In fact, five were damaged, and of these only three returned to Java. Return fire accounted for two Zeros.

From January 21 to 24, Japanese bombers kept up the pressure on Ambon. The final blow was delivered on January 24 when elements of the *Kido Butai* made their first appearance in the NEI. Carrier Division 2, composed of the carriers *Soryu* and *Hiryu*, launched a strike against Ambon on the previous day but it was aborted on account of the weather conditions. On the 24th, each carrier launched 27 aircraft (nine B5N2 level bombers, nine D3A1 dive-bombers, and nine Zeros) which pounded the port and airfield facilities. No Japanese aircraft were lost. The Allies were forced to abandon the airfield and use it only as an advanced landing ground.

The standard USAAF heavy bomber during the campaign was the B-17E. This was the latest version of the B-17 and first entered service in September 1941. It was heavily armed with up to ten .50-caliber machine guns. When flying in formation, the B-17 was an extremely hard target for the lightly armed Japanese fighters to deal with. This photo shows a group of 64th Sentai pilots with a captured B-17E on Java in March 1942. (Andrew Thomas Collection)

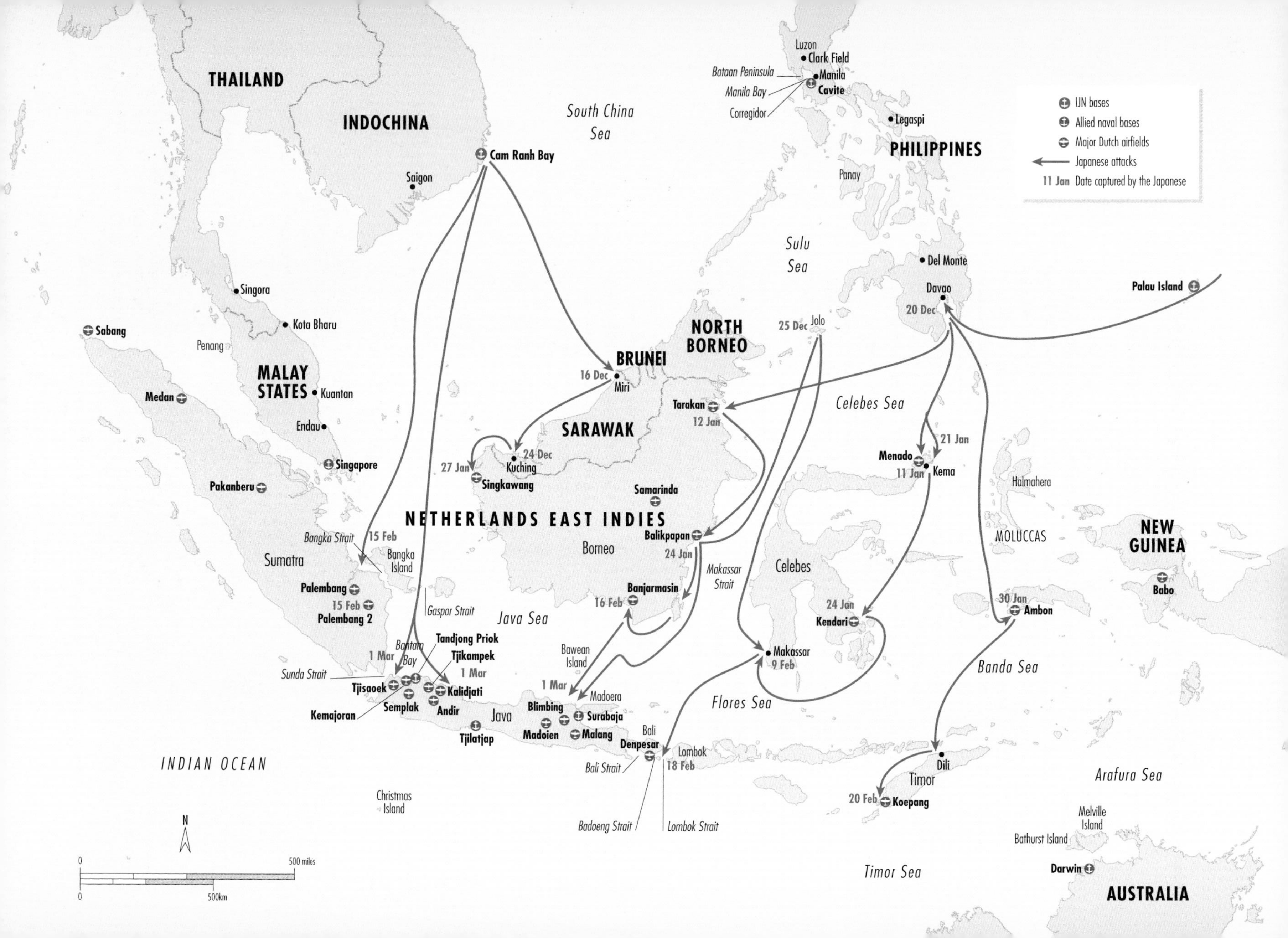

IJN bases
Allied naval bases
Major Dutch airfields
Japanese attacks
11 Jan Date captured by the Japanese
THAILAND
INDOCHINA
South China Sea
Cam Ranh Bay
Saigon
Luzon
Clark Field
Manila
Cavite
Bataan Peninsula
Manila Bay
Corregidor
Legaspi
PHILIPPINES
Panay
Sulu Sea
Del Monte
Davao
20 Dec
Palau Island
Singora
Kota Bharu
Penang
MALAY STATES
Kuantan
Endau
Singapore
Sabang
Medan
Pakanberu
Sumatra
NORTH BORNEO
BRUNEI
16 Dec
Miri
25 Dec
Jolo
Tarakan
12 Jan
SARAWAK
Celebes Sea
24 Dec
Kuching
27 Jan
Singkawang
Menado
11 Jan
21 Jan
Kema
Halmahera
Samarinda
NETHERLANDS EAST INDIES
Borneo
Balikpapan
24 Jan
Makassar Strait
Celebes
MOLUCCAS
NEW GUINEA
Babo
Bangka Strait
15 Feb
Bangka Island
Palembang
15 Feb
Palembang 2
Gaspar Strait
Java Sea
Banjarmasin
16 Feb
24 Jan
Kendari
30 Jan
Ambon
Tandjong Priok
Bantam Bay
Tjikampek
1 Mar
1 Mar
Sunda Strait
Tjisaoek
Kalidjati
Semplak
Andir
Kemajoran
Bawean Island
1 Mar
Madoera
Makassar
9 Feb
Banda Sea
Flores Sea
Blimbing
Surabaja
Java
Madoien
Malang
Tjilatjap
Bali
Denpesar
Lombok
18 Feb
Bali Strait
Badoeng Strait
Lombok Strait
Dili
Timor
20 Feb
Koepang
Arafura Sea
INDIAN OCEAN
Christmas Island
Melville Island
Bathurst Island
Darwin
Timor Sea
AUSTRALIA
N
0
500 miles
0
500km

OPPOSITE DUTCH AIRFIELDS IN THE NEI AND THE JAPANESE ADVANCE THROUGH THE NEI

Meanwhile, a Japanese reconnaissance aircraft spotted activity on Timor. On the morning of the 26th, six Zeros led by a C5M from the 3rd Air Group strafed the base at Koepang, accounting for two Dutch civil aircraft and a USAAF P-40E left behind when the 17th Pursuit Squadron came through the previous day.

On January 27, two B-17Es scored a rare success when they damaged seaplane tender *Sanuki Maru* off Balikpapan. The intercepting Zeros were unable to damage the big bombers. In return, six Zeros attacked Bandjermasin and caused major damage to the aircraft clustered there. A total of seven Martins were destroyed and two more damaged. A B-17 forced to land there two days earlier was also destroyed. The following day, Zeros destroyed two Buffalos at Samarinda. Only one Buffalo was left operational, so the base was evacuated.

Five B-17s returned to Balikpapan on January 29 to attack shipping. Four bombers were damaged by intense attacks from 13 Zeros which went on for 30 minutes. No Japanese ships were hit. Six more B-17Es returned to Balikpapan the following day. One was damaged, and again no damage was inflicted on the Japanese.

The Allied position was looking increasingly bleak. Japanese forces landed on Ambon against no Allied air or naval opposition on January 30. The Japanese moved more forces forward – 22 1st Air Group G3Ms to Menado and seven Kanoya G4Ms to Kendari. North of Java, only air bases at Bandjermasin in southern Borneo and Makassar on the Celebes were left operational to the Allies.

The battle for Sumatra

On January 18, the RAF established 225 (Bomber) Group on Sumatra to control the bombers being moved from Singapore and three new squadrons coming from India. At the end of the month, the group possessed 39 Hudsons from four squadrons and 28 Blenheim IVs from five squadrons. Two Hurricane squadrons, 232 and 258, departed Singapore and made up 226 (Fighter) Group. There were several airfields on Sumatra, but

B-17s in action

The USAAF used the B-17 heavy bomber to strike Japanese maritime targets throughout the campaign. Since these attacks were conducted from high altitude, they were rarely successful. An example of this occurred on February 19 when the B-17s were used to strike a Japanese convoy landing on Bali just to the east of Java. This was an important link in the air reinforcement route from Australia which had to be held. The Japanese convoy consisted of two transports, *Sasako Maru* and *Sagami Maru*, escorted by Asashio-class destroyers of the 8th Destroyer Division. As usual, the Allies were late in their response to a Japanese move. The convoy arrived at the anchorage off Sanur just after midnight on the 19th and began landing operations. The Japanese anticipated air attacks, which began after dawn. The first three aircraft to attack were three B-17Es from the 19th Bombardment Group. The aircraft arrived over the target singly. The first to attack did so just after 0700 hours and made two runs on what was claimed as a cruiser. A hit was claimed on the second run. Actually, the large Asashio-class destroyers were undamaged. This scene shows the second B-17E to arrive at about 0745 hours; it made several attempts to hit the convoy, which was now obscured by clouds. Four Tainan Air Group Zeros were providing air coverage for the convoy and these mounted a series of attacks on the lone B-17. The Americans claimed two shot down, but none was lost. The B-17 was forced to abort its mission and drop its bombs into the sea after its top turret ceased to function properly. The third B-17E attacked ten minutes later and dropped its bombs on a destroyer without success. Further heavy bomber attacks occurred throughout the morning against Zero opposition without success. Later in the day, two A-24s from the 91st Bomb Squadron avoided fighter opposition and placed a bomb on *Sagami Maru*, which temporarily brought it to a halt. The ship was later able to get under way on a single propeller. The Allies continued to attack the invasion convoy with a naval attack on the night of February 19–20; this was defeated by the outnumbered Japanese destroyer escort.

12498
Jim Laurier

the two most important were located on the southern part of the island near the city of Palembang. Palembang 1 (P1) was the main civilian airfield about 5 miles from Palembang and Palembang 2 (P2) was an airfield unknown to the Japanese some 20 miles to the south. There were also two major refineries and large oil fields in the area, which made it a primary target of the Japanese. The problem for the Allies was Palembang's vulnerability to seaborne attack. Though located well inland, it was located on the Moesi River which was navigable by ocean-going ships.

The Japanese prepared a large invasion force to seize Palembang consisting of 25 transports with a strong escort including *Ryujo*. The light carrier embarked 12 A5M4 fighters and 15 B5N1 attack aircraft. The invasion force departed Cam Ranh Bay in Indochina on February 10. Since the Allied ground defenses were very weak at Palembang, the only hope the Allies had was to repel the invasion by air or naval attack.

Before the invasion, the IJAAF planned a short but intense counterair campaign to gain air superiority. The Japanese spotted the buildup of aircraft at Palembang and made plans to strike. On February 6, the first attack was launched at P1 with 23 Ki-48s from the 75th and 90th Sentai escorted by 18 Ki-43s from the 64th Sentai and 14 from the 59th Sentai. Weather prevented the Japanese bombers from linking up with the fighters, but the Ki-43s pressed on. There was no radar warning, and the first warning by Observer Corps personnel gave the Hurricanes only a few minutes to respond. The defending fighters were thus unable to gain sufficient height for an interception and were caught as they were taking off. Four Hurricanes were lost, but three of the pilots returned to the airfield.

The following day the Japanese returned with another raid of six bombers escorted by 31 Ki-43s. The scenario of the previous day played out again. The British fighters received minimal warning and those inexperienced pilots who got off the ground were treated roughly by the Ki-43s. Three more Hurricanes were lost, but two pilots later returned to the airfield. There were a large number of aircraft present on the ground despite warning that such overcrowding on an airfield with no dispersal facilities was courting disaster. Japanese bombs accounted for six Blenheims and three Hurricanes destroyed and another 11 Hurricanes, one Buffalo, and one Hudson damaged. Another Blenheim was destroyed in the air when it was caught coming in to land just as the Japanese arrived. The only good news for the defenders was that the runway was undamaged and damage to support facilities was minor. Japanese records show they lost one Ki-43 and a bomber.

After this raid, P1 and P2 airfields finally received some antiaircraft guns, though their ammunition had not arrived. Eight 3.7in guns and six 40mm Bofors were sent to P1; four 3.7in and four 40mm were sent to P2, and a nearby oil facility received four 3.7in and four 40mm. The airfields remained almost devoid of ground defense personnel.

The Japanese returned for the third straight day on February 8. This raid consisted of 25 Ki-43s and 17 bombers. Two Hurricanes were on patrol when the Japanese arrived; both were shot down. After a break of several days, the IJAAF returned on February 13 with 29 Ki-43s and seven Ki-48s. P1 was the target again and this time the Observer Corps gave plenty of warning and an interception was made. The British claimed three fighters and two bombers. Actual Japanese losses were two fighters and a bomber. Only one Hurricane was lost.

The Allies were well aware of the approach of the Japanese invasion convoy aimed at Palembang. The Battle of Bangka Strait began on February 14 with a major British air attack with all 15 operational Hurricanes from 232 and 258 Squadrons from P1 escorting 15 Blenheims from P2.

Preceding the main strike were five Hudsons from 8 RAAF Squadron. Only three attacked, but had no success. Six Hudsons of 1 RAAF Squadron attacked next. These encountered Zeros over the convoy which shot down one Hudson, made another crash-land on P1, and badly damaged another. The aircrews claimed hits on three transports. Five more Hudsons followed, but were again attacked by Zeros. One RAAF Hudson was shot down, but the

The Initial Japanese Air Attack on Eastern Java – February 3, 1942

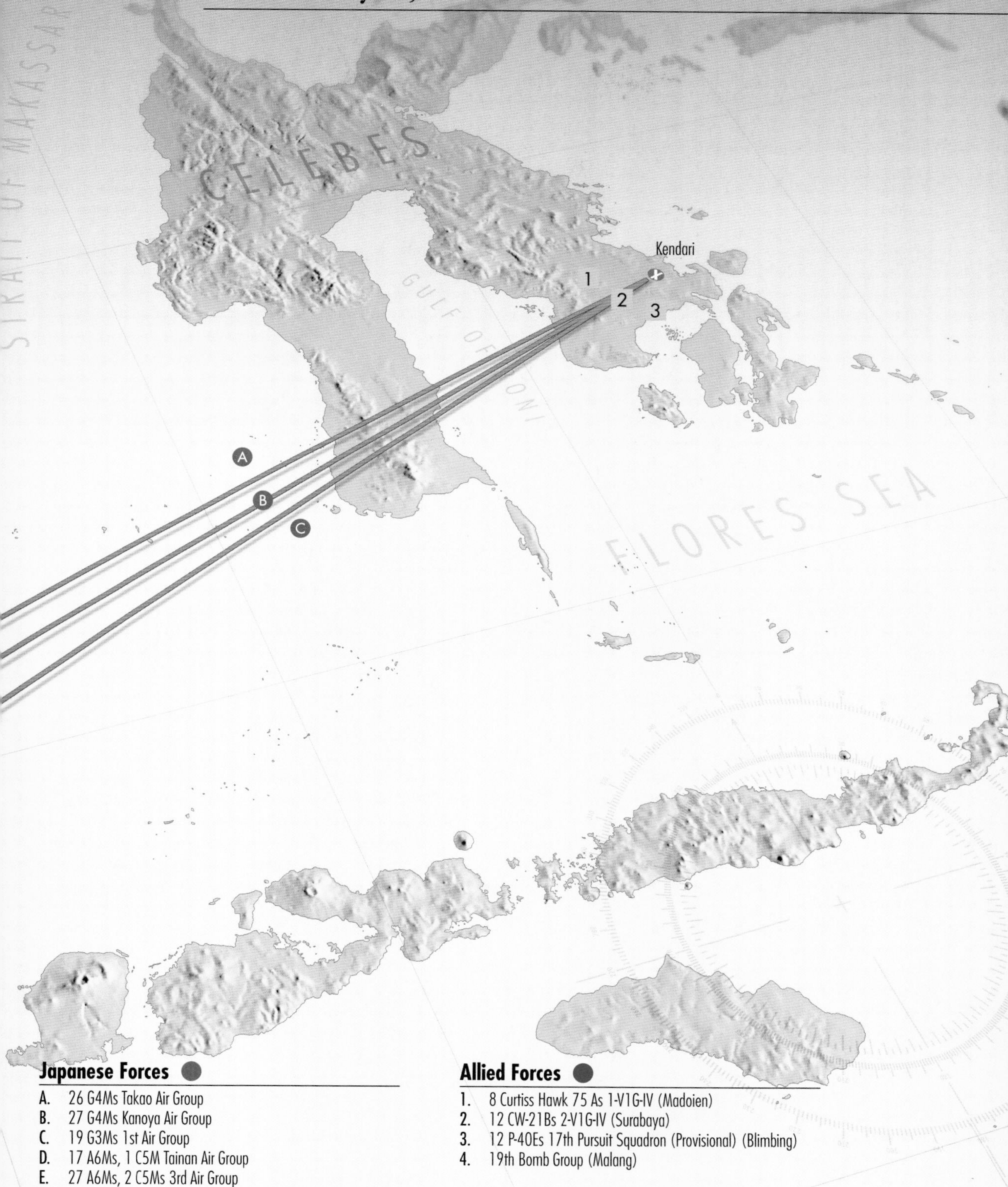

Japanese Forces

A. 26 G4Ms Takao Air Group
B. 27 G4Ms Kanoya Air Group
C. 19 G3Ms 1st Air Group
D. 17 A6Ms, 1 C5M Tainan Air Group
E. 27 A6Ms, 2 C5Ms 3rd Air Group

Allied Forces

1. 8 Curtiss Hawk 75 As 1-V1G-IV (Madoien)
2. 12 CW-21Bs 2-V1G-IV (Surabaya)
3. 12 P-40Es 17th Pursuit Squadron (Provisional) (Blimbing)
4. 19th Bomb Group (Malang)

The IJNAF strike of February 4, 1942 with 60 bombers directed at the CSF could not replicate the success of December 10 against Force Z. On this day, the Japanese bombers carried no torpedoes so had to rely on horizontal bombing only. They were able to hit *Houston* with a 550lb bomb and light cruiser *Marblehead* with two 132lb bombs. This photo shows part of the resulting damage to *Marblehead*. In addition to the damage shown, the cruiser had a hole on its bow which could not be repaired locally. The ship was ordered back to the United States for permanent repairs. (Naval History and Heritage Command)

The invasion of Java was scheduled for late February. To create the required condition of air superiority over eastern Java and to complete the destruction of the CSF, the Japanese stepped up air operations. On February 5, the IJNAF returned to the skies over Surabaya. Twenty-seven Zeros and a C5M of the Tainan Air Group were intercepted by the four remaining CW-21Bs. Two of the Dutch fighters were forced to crash-land. The Zeros also encountered a strike of B-17s headed for Balikpapan and attacked. One bomber was damaged and the mission was aborted. The first wave was followed by 11 Zeros and a C5M of the 3rd Air Group. These encountered the last two Hawks and shot both down, as well as a Dutch Catalina. These Zeros also went on to down to strafe the flying boat base. In this very effective attack, three Do 24s, as well as two Dutch and two USN Catalinas were destroyed.

More bad news followed for the Allies. On the same day, 23 Kanoya and eight Takao bombers attacked Denpasar Airfield on Bali. The bombers were escorted by ten Zeros from 3rd Air Group. This installation was important since it was part of the pipeline used to funnel air reinforcements from Australia to Java. The attack found 12 USAAF P-40s present. Ten P-40Es succeeded in getting airborne but the Zeros made short work of the inexperienced 20th Pursuit Squadron. Five P-40s were destroyed by air combat and two more by bombs; three more were damaged.

On February 8, nine B-17Es of 7th Bomb Group attempted to bomb Kendari. One bomber aborted, and the remaining aircraft ran into nine Tainan Air Group Zeros. In the most effective attack of the campaign against a B-17 formation, the Japanese made a head-on approach. Two bombers were immediately shot down and in a series of attacks four others were heavily damaged. No Zeros were even damaged.

The Takao Air Group returned to Surabaya on February 18. A *chutai* of 21 bombers failed to rendezvous with the escorting Zeros from the Tainan Air Group and went into the target area unescorted. The bombers were hit by 12 P-40Es from the 17th Pursuit Squadron. The P-40s claimed a total of eight bombers. Actual Japanese losses were two bombers lost to the P-40s and another to antiaircraft fire. Another was forced to ditch on the way home because of battle damage. This was one of the few instances of heavy IJNAF bomber losses during the campaign.

February 19 was another day of unrelenting disaster for the Allies. Most importantly, 188 aircraft from four carriers of the *Kido Butai* hit Darwin. The carrier aircraft plastered shore facilities and sank nine ships in the harbor. Fifty-four bombers from Kendari then attacked two nearby airfields. The major link in Australia to the NEI had been temporarily neutralized.

The Japanese had dispatched a small invasion force to occupy Bali just to the east of Java. The invasion was covered by a small number of Tainan Air Group Zeros. Just two Zeros fought doggedly against four heavy bomber attacks between 0500 and 0800 hours. Both Zeros were damaged, but none of the USAAF bombers hit their targets. In their most effective operation of the campaign, two A-24s of the ill-fated 91st Bomb Squadron got through the Zeros and placed a bomb on a transport. Bali was captured after a short fight, which began on the evening of February 18. The Japanese Bali invasion force was also attacked by Allied naval forces on the night of February 19–20. The four IJN destroyers present defeated a much larger Allied force. The invasion of Bali was the only instance during the campaign when a Japanese invasion was not properly covered by air and naval forces. Even in this instance, the Allies were unable to make the Japanese pay for their rashness. Combined with the invasion of Timor on February 20, which was captured after a three-day fight, the air transfer route from Australia to Java was cut.

More bad news for the Allies came from Malang Airfield, which was hit by 18 bombers and 23 Tainan Air Group Zeros. The bombers diverted to another target because of weather, but the Zeros pressed on. USAAF P-40s rose to intercept but were routed. For the cost of a single Zero, seven American fighters went down.

Despite the severe attrition inflicted on the Allied air forces on Java, the Japanese were not happy with the results of their counterair campaign. On February 23, they decided to

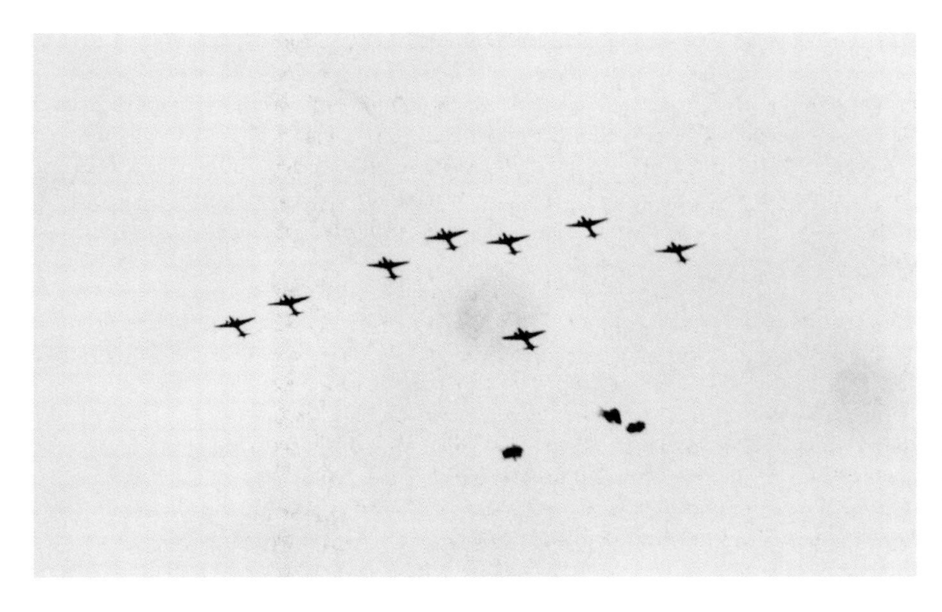

The Japanese were known for their impeccable formation flying during bombing runs. Usually attacks were conducted by a *chutai* of nine bombers and sometimes by a formation of two or three *chutai*. This *chutai* of G4M bombers is not in the usual 'V' formation, with only eight bombers present and one of those out of position. The accuracy of Japanese bombing attacks was usually good, and sometimes outstanding. It was certainly better than Allied bombing attacks on the average. (Australian War Memorial)

The harbor and naval base at Surabaya were prime targets and during the last half of February were subjected to nearly daily raids. This is the aftermath of one such raid. Despite this chaos, the naval base remained operative until the end of the campaign. (Australian War Memorial)

delay the invasion by two days until February 28. The inability of the IJNAF to neutralize the CSF was of even greater concern. Hoping to hit the CSF in harbor, the Japanese sent 51 bombers to Surabaya on the 24th, 22 on the 25th, and 26 on the 26th; each strike was escorted by nine Zeros. Allied attempts to intercept the raids were unsuccessful and resulted in further fighter attrition.

When the CSF departed Surabaya to attack the invasion convoy for eastern Java carrying the 48th Division, the IJNAF was unable to respond. On February 27, the Genzan Air Group was stuck on the ground at Kuching due to fog. The lack of fuel and munitions curtailed operations. Only eight Kanoya G4Ms were launched against the CSF in the afternoon and these carried only small 132lb bombs because nothing else was available. The bombers failed to hit their target. That afternoon and evening in the battle of the Java Sea, the CSF was decisively defeated by IJN surface forces.

Also on February 27, the IJNAF scored another important success. The seaplane tender *Langley*, formerly the USN's first aircraft carrier, was spotted headed for Tjilatjap on southern Java with a cargo of P-40s. Sixteen Takao G4M bombers from Bali were dispatched to attack. The first wave of seven bombers missed this slow target, but the next *chutai* of nine aircraft delivered their loads with impressive accuracy scoring five hits and three near misses. The ship was later scuttled.

The final battle for Java

The battle for air control over Java was a foregone conclusion since the Allied Combined Chiefs of Staff had decided on February 22 that Java could not be defended and that no more units would be sent to reinforce the island's defenses. Those forces already on the island would fight it out. Remaining Allied air forces on Java were brought under a new command called Java Air Command (JAC) under Dutch Major General L. H. Peirse. JAC consisted of three national headquarters controlling British and Australian, American, and Dutch units. There was also a small staff to control the remaining MLD flying boats. The primary objective of JAC and the CSF was to prevent an invasion of Java. By this point in

The 90th Sentai Ki-48s followed up by bombing the hangars. Two USAAF B-17s were caught on the ground; one was destroyed and one heavily damaged. The Japanese lost one Ki-43 and its experienced pilot, and one more was written off after it returned to Palembang. One more Ki-43 was lost attacking a pair of transiting B-17s encountered in flight. One of the bombers was also lost. By the end of the first day, the Dutch and British were down to 29 operational fighters in western Java.

The next day, the Japanese raided Kalidjati with 24 Ki-43s and ten Ki-48s. The raid was not intercepted and the Ki-48s dropped their loads which destroyed two Dutch bombers, and damaged two more, one heavily. RAF Hurricanes from Tjililitan managed to shoot down one Japanese reconnaissance plane among the several which were active during the day.

The Japanese maintained the pressure on February 21. The Allies began the day with 29 operational fighters. The Japanese mounted a major effort with 29 Ki-43s escorting 15 light bombers from the 90th Sentai. Twelve Ki-43s went astray in bad weather and the Dutch used a height advantage to conduct a diving attack against the surprised Japanese. The Dutch held their own and destroyed one Ki-43, and another crashed after running out of fuel on the way back to Palembang. Dutch losses were comparatively light with one Buffalo and one CW-21B. Two more Buffalos were badly damaged. Two Ki-48s were destroyed by antiaircraft fire when they attacked Kalidjati

Two raids were conducted on February 22. With a total of 15 Ki-48 light bombers escorted by 26 Ki-43 fighters, Kemajoran and Semplak Airfields were attacked. Allied fighters did not make an interception since they were assigned to convoy protection. The airfields lacked antiaircraft protection and the Japanese bombers delivered some serious blows. At Kemajoran, several Allied bombers were caught on the ground and damaged. At Semplak, the toll was much higher; six Hudsons were destroyed on the ground and three more were written off after heavy damage. Also on this day, command of Allied air forces on Java was transferred to Dutch Major General L. H. Van Oyen. Going forward he declined to commit fighters offensively over Sumatra in favor of focusing on air defense.

The inability of the Allies to defend their airfields was a continuing, and eventually crippling, factor in the campaign. Many more Allied aircraft were destroyed on the ground than in the air. Here a USAAF B-17 is shown burning after a Japanese strike against the Dutch airfield at Andir on eastern Java. (Netherlands Institute for Military History)

The following day, Japanese activity was limited by poor weather. The Allies moved their six remaining Hudsons to Kalidjati since it was better protected. All considered, the Allied counterair campaign over western Java and Palembang was not a total failure since it contributed to the Japanese decision on February 23 to delay the invasion of western Java two days until February 28. The IJAAF claimed that Allied air power based in western Java had been eliminated, but the IJN disagreed and did not want to conduct the invasion with only tenuous air control.

To finish off Allied air power, the Japanese intensified counterair operations on February 24. At this time, the Allies possessed 35 operational fighters. Three airfields were attacked and the Japanese met resistance from Dutch Buffalos and CW-21Bs and from RAF Hurricanes. Andir Airfield was subjected to an attack from 17 Ki-48s escorted by 14 Ki-43s from the 59th Sentai. They were intercepted by nine Dutch fighters; the air-to-air battle was a draw with both sides losing a fighter, but the bombers pressed on to the airfield and dropped their payloads, accounting for three B-17s damaged and one Dutch bomber destroyed and another damaged. Another large raid was sent against Kalidjati, consisting of 16 75th Sentai Ki-48s escorted by 13 64th Sentai Ki-43s. The raid was not intercepted and proceeded to bomb and strafe the airfield. Two Hudsons were destroyed and several more suffered light damage and the airfield was temporarily closed; three Ki-48s were shot down by antiaircraft fire. Over Tjililitan Airfield, British Hurricanes were able to make an interception, but lost two aircraft at the hands of the Ki-43s. One Japanese bomber was destroyed by antiaircraft fire. Total losses for the Japanese were heavy with five bombers and a fighter lost; in addition to the aircraft lost on the ground, Allied fighter losses were also heavy with one Dutch fighter and four RAF Hurricanes lost.

The 25th was the last day of Japanese counterair operations over western Java. It also saw the first and last raid conducted by the IJNAF over western Java. The IJAAF focused on Kalidjati and accounted for three Dutch Hurricanes in the air and two RAF Blenheims on the ground. In exchange, one Ki-43 and two Ki-48s were lost. The IJNAF committed 27 G3Ms escorted by 13 Zeros and accompanied by a single C5M reconnaissance aircraft against Tandjong Priok Harbor and nearby Tjililitan Airfield. The raid was intercepted by eight Hurricanes; in the ensuing melee two Hurricanes went down but the RAF also accounted for a Zero. Antiaircraft fire destroyed the C5M. The Japanese bombers were not intercepted as they headed to the harbor. The attack damaged a British tanker, but 11 of the 27 G3Ms were damaged by antiaircraft fire.

On February 25, Allied flying boats discovered a Japanese invasion force anchored off Balikpapan. This was the force intended for eastern Java. The location of the invasion force intended for western Java was unknown, but intelligence indicated that such a force was being prepared. The CSF was sent to engage the eastern invasion force. Allied air efforts were devoted to finding the western invasion force and attacking the eastern invasion force.

The failure of the CSF and of weak Allied air attacks meant the Japanese landed on eastern Java near Kragen and at three locations on western Java. One of the landing sites in western Java was near the important air base at Kalidjati. Once ashore, the Japanese pressed the attack. The major Dutch effort to repel the invasion on land was made at Kalidjati. The battle for the air base extended from February 28 to March 3 and forced the Dutch to fall back to the Bandoeng plateau. The Japanese gained access to the plateau through the Tjiater Pass in a clash fought between March 5 and 7. The Allied forces on Java surrendered on March 9. Before the final surrender, the various Allied air forces began to flee Java. The USAAF withdrew its remaining B-17s on March 1. The final operations by the Dutch air forces were conducted on March 7 and the last RAF aircraft left Java the following day. Aside from mopping-up operations, the Japanese conquest of the NEI was complete.

ANALYSIS AND CONCLUSION

The four-month air campaign for Malaya and the NEI resulted in an overwhelming Allied defeat. There were several reasons for this debacle. First and foremost, the Japanese had an overwhelming numerical advantage. The combined IJNAF and IJAAF air forces began the campaign with over 800 aircraft. In comparison, the Allied air forces were much weaker. The RAF began the campaign in Malaya with an operational strength of 158 aircraft and the Dutch possessed some 230 operational aircraft. Almost all of these aircraft were obsolescent or obsolete. Furthermore, the Allies were unable to establish a steady stream of reinforcements.

In addition to their overwhelming numerical advantage, the Japanese had better aircraft and more experienced aircrews. The standard IJNAF fighter, the A6M Zero, was the pre-eminent air superiority fighter of the opening stages of the Pacific War. Its long range, fairly heavy armament, and maneuverability made it well suited for the campaign which the Japanese intended to fight in Southeast Asia. The Japanese Navy's bombers, the G3M and G4M, were also ideally suited to the campaign since both types possessed long range, which was a critical factor given the expanse of the area and the relatively few airfields available. The inability of these bombers, and even of the formidable Zero, to sustain significant combat damage, was not exposed during the campaign. Only when the IJNAF met an equally determined and well-equipped defender in the air over Guadalcanal were the shortcomings of the IJNAF's land-based air force fully revealed.

A comprehensive account of IJNAF losses during the campaign is difficult to provide. What seems clear is that they were generally light, and those aircraft which were lost were quickly replaced. The principal air units were able to maintain their strength throughout the campaign. An example of the scale of losses is provided from the records of the 22nd Air Flotilla, which during the period from December 29 to January 22 lost two bombers, five Zeros, and one C5M. Two additional bombers force-landed and one was lost for operational reasons. The entire IJNAF force committed to the Southern Operation lost only 38 aircraft during the period January 4 to April 6. This included 14 bombers, six reconnaissance aircraft,

The Mitsubishi G4M was the best Japanese bomber of the campaign. It had a respectable top speed, bomb load, and defensive armament, and also possessed an enormous range for a medium bomber. It did have a significant weakness which was not revealed during the campaign. This is a G4M1 of the Kanoya Air Group in 1942. (NARA)

The outstanding fighter of the campaign was the Mitsubishi A6M2 Type O fighter. This is an aircraft of the 3rd Air Group photographed at Rabaul just after the conclusion of the NEI campaign. The Zero possessed an unbeatable combination of range, armament, maneuverability, and climbing ability when matched with an experienced pilot. (Yasuho Izawa Collection)

16 fighters, and two flying boats. This was from all causes, and many of these were lost for operational reasons, not to enemy action.

The IJNAF accomplished a great deal in a fairly short period of time. The entire conquest of Malaya, Singapore, and the NEI was covered by only three fighter units which never possessed more than 115 Zeros. These were the primary spearheads of the Japanese advance. The principal reason for their success was the extremely high quality of their pilots. Almost all had received rigorous prewar training and many had the benefit of combat experience over China. They were the cream of the IJNAF. Fourteen of the top 26 fighter aces during the war served in Malaya and the NEI, including three of the top four aces.

The strike aircraft were also impressive as demonstrated by their destruction of Force Z early in the campaign. The bombers were never able to replicate this feat against the CSF, but it should be kept in mind that two of the CSF's major operations were thwarted by the application of Japanese air power. Against weak fighter and antiaircraft defenses, the IJNAF's fighters and bombers roamed the theater striking Allied land-based installations inflicting unsustainable attrition on Allied air forces.

While the IJNAF usually gets most of the credit for the Japanese victories in Malaya and the NEI, the IJAAF also played an essential role. It demonstrated the viability of its counterair doctrine when it crushed the RAF in northern Malaya in a matter of two days. The IJAAF covered the breakneck Japanese advance down the Malayan peninsula and never lost the initiative to the RAF. The 3rd Air Division was able to accomplish all of its missions. It played the principal role in reducing the RAF in Singapore and Sumatra, and then inflicted sufficient attrition on Allied air forces in western Java to permit the invasion of the island to proceed largely unimpeded by air attack. The IJAAF was susceptible to the same kind of attacks it was carrying out against RAF air bases since the Japanese did not possess radar. The RAF, USAAF, and ML-KNIL all attempted to carry out a campaign against major Japanese airfields, but lacked the aircraft to sustain it.

IJAAF aircraft used in the campaign were a mixed bag which did not compare favorably to the IJNAF's. The Ki-43 fighter is overlooked since it did not enjoy the early-war fame of the Zero. Nevertheless, the Ki-43 was a nimble fighter with excellent range. It was certainly better than most of the Allied fighters it was pitted against. It should be remembered that the IJAAF offensive was led by only two *sentai* of Ki-43 which flew almost continuously for the duration of the campaign. Many IJAAF pilots were combat veterans, giving them an edge over their Allied counterparts. Six of the IJAAF's 22 top aces of the war served in Malaya and the NEI.

IJAAF bombers, primarily the Ki-21 "heavy" bomber and the Ki-48 light bomber, were mediocre aircraft even when compared to the collection of obsolescent bombers deployed to the region by the Allies. Nevertheless, they proved rugged and easy to maintain. Against weak air defenses, they were more than capable of dealing heavy blows to Allied installations, which they did repeatedly during the campaign. Not long after this, the same aircraft proved ineffective against more modern opponents in Burma and New Guinea.

The RAF fought bravely, but not effectively. In Malaya, it was deployed to airfields which were difficult to defend. These were too far forward and not defended by antiaircraft guns. Even the airfields on Singapore were not protected against enemy attack, which meant that all offensive aircraft had to be withdrawn to the NEI later in the campaign. The numbers of aircraft were simply inadequate to accomplish the RAF's dual primary missions of air defense and maritime strike.

A post-campaign RAF critique highlighted some of the RAF's principal shortcomings. These included inadequate fighter and antiaircraft defenses, the inability of peacetime stations to withstand air attack, and a paucity of adequate early-warning systems. This summed up the situation on December 8–9, 1941 and explained how the RAF lost the battle for northern Malaya in two days. Of the 110 RAF aircraft committed, only 50 remained operational after the first day. At the end of the second day, there were only ten aircraft left operational and Pulford withdrew all but two squadrons to Singapore. To be fair, even if the conditions listed above had been corrected before the start of the war, the RAF would still have lost the battle for air superiority, but it would have taken more than two days.

RAF aircraft were generally obsolescent, and this was an important factor during the campaign. The standard RAF fighter was the Buffalo, universally acknowledged as one of the worst fighters of the war. The four squadrons equipped with this aircraft were also handicapped by inexperienced pilots and ground crews and a lack of spare parts. The Hurricane was a marked improvement and once their pilots gained some experience, the RAF was able to hold its own against the IJAAF over western Java.

Offensive aircraft were deficient in both quantity and quality. The light bomber force, composed of Bristol Blenheims and Lockheed Hudsons, possessed neither the speed nor

The Ki-43 spearheaded the IJAAF's advance into Malaya and then the NEI. It was an extremely maneuverable fighter but had a weak armament of only two 7.7mm machine guns and was devoid of armor and self-sealing fuel tanks. Top speed was 308mph, comparable to Allied fighters, but the light weight of the Ki-43 gave it impressive climbing capabilities. Allied pilots were unaware of the IJAAF's new fighter and invariably reported encounters with the Ki-43 as Zeros since the two types did have a basically similar appearance. (Andrew Thomas Collection)

protection to operate in contested air space. The primary weapon to attack Japanese shipping was the Vickers Vildebeest torpedo bomber. This antiquated aircraft should not have been in front-line service and only confirmed the second-class status of RAF units in the Far East. It is damning that during the entire campaign RAF aircraft sank only two Japanese merchant ships.

The Dutch Air Force fought bravely but also suffered defeat after defeat. This was not unexpected since the main Dutch fighter was the ill-fated Buffalo, while none of the Dutch fighter pilots had any operational or combat experience and many were new to fighters. The primary Dutch bomber was obsolete and also proved unable to operate in contested air space without heavy losses. The Dutch pressed their attacks against Japanese shipping bravely, but their ability to hit maritime targets was limited, as shown by the fact that during the entire campaign Dutch bombers sank only one minesweeper and two transports. The Dutch naval air force was efficient but lacked the aircraft to successfully attack defended targets. It did sink a destroyer, which was the largest Japanese combatant sunk by any Allied air force.

The only way the air campaign for the NEI might have unfolded differently was if the USAAF had been able to move onto Java earlier and in strength. But USAAF plans to accomplish this were nothing more than fantasy. Only a small number of American aircraft ever made it to the NEI and these were too few and too late to have a significant impact.

The American bomber force was the first to fight and had the greatest potential to impact the campaign. Bombing from high altitude as prescribed by doctrine, the bombers were totally ineffective in a maritime strike role. No Japanese ship was sunk by heavy bomber attack during the campaign. As the pace of the Japanese advance picked up, the American bomber force operated on an increasingly reactive basis. During the period from January 22 to February 3, the bomber force flew 15 missions to widely separated targets. Of the 84 bombers on these missions, 17 were aborted because of the weather conditions and another 29 flew missions with no results. Of the five missions and 38 bombers which struck targets, only two transports and two other ships were claimed; in fact, no hits were achieved. In return, bomber losses were heavy, mainly owing to operational factors.

Bad weather precluded any successful heavy bomber missions in early February. On February 8, nine B-17s were sent to hit the Japanese airfield at Kendari. The formation was scattered because of poor weather and when nine Zeros attacked, they scored heavily against the heavy bombers for the only time in the campaign. From February 9–18, the bomber force intensified operations with 16 missions with 72 B-17 and 15 LB-30 sorties. Of these, 51 sorties were scrubbed because of poor weather or for mechanical reasons. Claims were made for four ships hit, including a cruiser, but all these claims were unfounded. Given the heavy bombers' ineffectiveness in the maritime strike role, a better course of action would have been to have selected a key Japanese land target for sustained attack, like Kendari Airfield after its capture by the Japanese.

The USAAF's fighter force operated the best Allied fighter of the campaign but did so with inexperienced pilots. The American fighters, like all Allied fighters, were hampered by an infrastructure that featured weak early-warning systems and little to no antiaircraft protection at airfields. The operations of all American squadrons were also hampered by lack of maintenance personnel and spare parts.

The victories of Japanese air power in Southeast Asia during the first four months of the war were truly shocking. Against multiple opponents, the IJNAF and IJAAF had gained an overwhelming series of successes. All too soon, the weaknesses of Japanese air power which were not revealed over Malaya or the NEI would be fully exposed. Japan's inability to fight a battle of attrition with the Allies, replace experienced pilots, or field significantly improved aircraft would prove fatal. Like the Allies in the opening days of air combat over Southeast Asia, the IJNAF and IJAAF were destined to fight brave but futile battles to overcome overwhelming numerical odds with obsolescent or obsolete aircraft.

BIBLIOGRAPHY

Boer, P. C., *The Loss of Java*, NUS Press, Singapore (2011)

Clayton, Graham, *Last Stand in Singapore*, Random House New Zealand, Auckland (2008)

Craven, Wesley and Cate, James, *The Army Air Forces in World War II, Volume One*, Office of the Air Force History, Washington, DC (1983)

Cull, Brian, *Buffalos over Singapore*, Grub Street, London (2003)

Cull, Brian, *Hurricanes over Singapore*, Grub Street, London (2004)

Farrell, Brian, *The Defence and Fall of Singapore 1940–1942*, Tempus Publishing, Stroud (2005)

Ferkl, Martin, *Mitsubishi G4M Betty*, REVI Publications, Ostrave, Czech Republic (2002)

Foreign Histories Division, General Headquarters Far East Command, *Japanese Monograph No. 31, Southern Air Operations Record 1941–1945*, Tokyo (n.d.)

Foreign Histories Division, General Headquarters Far East Command, *Japanese Monograph No. 69, Java–Sumatra Area Air Operations Record, December 1941–March 1942*, Tokyo (1946)

Foreign Histories Division, General Headquarters Far East Command, *Japanese Monograph No. 101, Naval Operations in the Invasion of Netherlands East Indies December 1941–March 1942*, Tokyo (1950)

Francillon, René, *Japanese Aircraft of the Pacific War*, Naval Institute Press, Annapolis, Maryland (1979)

Gillison, Douglas, *Royal Australian Air Force 1939–1942*, Australian War Memorial, Canberra (1962)

Hata, Ikuhiko, Izawa, Yasuho and Shores, Christopher, *Japanese Army Air Force Fighter Units and Their Aces 1931–1945*, Grub Street, London (2002)

Hata, Ikuhiko, Izawa, Yasuho and Shores, Christopher, *Japanese Naval Air Force Fighter Units and Their Aces 1932–1945*, Grub Street, London (2011)

Ichimura, Hiroshi, *Ki-43 'Oscar' Aces of World War 2*, Osprey Publishing, Oxford (2009)

Kelly, Terence, *Hurricanes over the Jungle*, Pen & Sword Aviation, Barnsley (2005)

Kirby, S. Woodburn, *The War Against Japan, Volume 1*, HMSO, London (1957)

Kreis, John, *Air Warfare and Air Base Air Defense*, Office of the Air Force History, Washington, DC (1988)

Lake, Jon, *Blenheim Squadrons of World War 2*, Osprey Publishing, Oxford (1998)

Lohnstein, Marc, *Royal Netherlands East Indies Army 1936–42*, Osprey Publishing, Oxford (2018)

Millman, Nicholas, *Ki-27 'Nate' Aces*, Osprey Publishing, Oxford (2013)

Morison, Samuel E., *The Rising Sun in the Pacific, Volume Three, History of United States Naval Operations in World War II*, Little, Brown and Company, Boston (1975)

Peattie, Mark, *Sunburst*, Naval Institute Press, Annapolis, Maryland (2001)

Richards, Denis and Saunders, Hilary St. George, *Royal Air Force 1939–1945, Volume 2*, HMSO, London (1974)

Robinson, Neil, *Pearl Harbor to Coral Sea the First Six Months of the Pacific War*, AIRfile Publications Ltd, Barnsley (2011)

Rohwer, Jurgen, *Chronology of the War at Sea 1939–1945* (third ed.), Naval Institute Press, Annapolis, Maryland (2005)

Salecker, Gene, *Fortress Against the Sun*, Combined Publishing, Conshohocken, Pennsylvania (2001)

Shores, Christopher, Cull, Brian and Izawa, Yasuho, *Bloody Shambles, Volume 1*, Grub Street, London (1992)

Shores, Christopher, Cull, Brian and Izawa, Yasuho, *Bloody Shambles, Volume 2*, Grub Street, London (1993)

Stenman, Kari and Thomas, Andrew, *Brewster F2A Buffalo Aces of World War 2*, Osprey Publishing, Oxford (2010)
Stille, Mark, *Java Sea 1942*, Osprey Publishing, Oxford (2019)
Stille, Mark, *Malaya and Singapore 1941–42*, Osprey Publishing, Oxford (2016)
War History Office of the National Defense College of Japan, *The Invasion of the Dutch East Indies*, Leiden University Press (2015)
War History Office of the National Defense College of Japan, *The Operations of the Navy in the Dutch East Indies and the Bay of Bengal*, Leiden University Press, Leiden (2018)
Womack, Tom, *The Allied Defense of the Malay Barrier, 1941–1942*, McFarland & Company, Jefferson, North Carolina (2016)
Womack, Tom, *The Dutch Naval Air Force Against Japan*, McFarland & Company, Jefferson, North Carolina (2006)

INDEX

Note: page locators in **bold** refer to illustrations, captions, and plates. All hardware is Japanese unless otherwise stated.